MW01116132

THIS BOOK WAS SELF-PUBLISHED

A TECHNICAL GUIDE

MICHAEL BAZZELL

This Book Was Self-Published:
A Technical Guide

ISBN: 978-0-578-74438-4

Project Editors: Ashley Martin, M.S. Williams, D. Sapp

First Published: September 2020

The information in this book is distributed on an "As Is" basis, without warranty. The author has taken great care in preparation of this book, but assumes no responsibility for errors or omissions. No liability is assumed for incidental or consequential damages in connection with or arising out of the use of the information or programs contained herein.

Rather than use a trademark symbol with every occurrence of a trademarked name, this book uses the names only in an editorial fashion and to the benefit of the trademark owner, with no intention of infringement of the trademark.

Due to the use of quotation marks to identify specific text to be used as search queries and data entry, the author has chosen to display the British rule of punctuation outside of quotes. This ensures that the quoted content is accurate for replication. To maintain consistency, this format is continued throughout the entire book.

The technology referenced in this book was edited and verified by a professional team for accuracy. Exact tutorials in reference to websites, software, and hardware configurations change rapidly. All tutorials in this book were confirmed accurate as of August 1, 2020. Readers may find slight discrepancies within the methods as technology changes.

CONTENTS

ABOUT THE AUTHOR

MICHAEL BAZZELL

Michael Bazzell investigated computer crimes on behalf of the government for over 20 years. As a side-hustle, he has self-published eighteen books since 2012. After leaving government work, he served as the technical advisor for the first season of the television hacker drama *Mr. Robot*. His books *Open Source Intelligence Techniques* and *Extreme Privacy* have become training manuals for intelligence gathering and privacy hardening within both government and private sector communities. Both titles continue to sell thousands of copies annually. He now hosts the weekly *Privacy, Security, and OSINT Show*, and assists individual clients in achieving ultimate privacy, both proactively and as a response to an undesired situation.

INTRODUCTION

Simply stated, this book is about this book. I should probably back up a bit.

In 2005, I experienced my first taste of published writing. I created a series of articles for *Law & Order Magazine* through Hendon Publishing. It was the first time I saw my name in print as a writer for an official magazine with glossy pages and a professional layout. This lit a fire that I still feel today. Throughout 2007 and 2008, I continued writing, but started using a pseudonym. I submitted articles to *2600: The Hacker Quarterly*, which were all published. I was an active cyber-crime investigator for the FBI at the time, and I had concerns about using my real name associated with anything including the term "hacker" in the title. The magazine was legal and could be purchased in most major bookstores, but I wasn't taking any chances.

Around this time, I was bitten by the book-writing bug. I worked with a traditional publisher and continued to use a pseudonym. I was offered a contract to write a technical manual associated with computer security which would be used as required text for first-year college courses. I was a hired gun. I was paid $1,500 and couldn't believe my luck. After completing the project, I determined that I was paid an average of $9.00 per hour, and the publisher was likely making a ton of money from book sales within college bookstores. I received a valuable education.

I decided that I wanted to write my own book on my terms. I created a proposal for a book about online investigations and eagerly submitted it to dozens of publishers. All of them declined. Most of them never acknowledged receipt of the proposal. A few responded with a canned message stating they were not interested. Only one responded in a helpful way. Bill Pollack, the CEO of No Starch Press, sent me an email confirming he had received my proposal. He was clear that he would not contract the book, but offered a ton of helpful advice and guidance. He also mailed me a free copy of a book his company had recently published which he thought could be helpful. I studied the content, formatting, design, and anything else I could suck up from this kind gesture. A few years later, my original proposal became my first self-published book titled *Open Source Intelligence Techniques*. It is currently in its seventh edition and has sold over 70,000 copies. Without Bill's blunt honesty, it would have never been completed.

Since then, I have self-published eighteen books, including this one, and contracted two books with traditional publishers under pseudonyms. While I now have contacts within the traditional publishing community interested in my books, I prefer to self-publish every new title. My previous books were all related to computer security, privacy, and online investigations. This title forces me to leave my comfort zone. I have considered writing a book about the self-publishing process since I first discovered the option, but assumed the market for this topic was already saturated. In the past year, two episodes of my podcast were devoted to this topic, which were well-received and had some of the highest listener downloads of all shows. I revisited the current landscape of self-publishing books, and found most of them to focus on marketing, promotion, and money.

I was unable to locate any books which explained the difference between interior PDF/X-1a:2001 and PDF/X-3:2002 formats and reasons why the former is the best to use for final proof-ready documents. None of the books identified the benefits and risks of choosing "Expanded Distribution" for a project, or the limitations of "Independently Published" titles issued exclusively by Amazon. I was unable to find a book which clearly explained the nuances of free and paid ISBNs and the strategy of using both to ensure my titles were available to every library and bookstore in the world, while maximizing my royalties for copies sold on Amazon. In my mind, these were very important aspects of creating my own product which seem to have been ignored. These were the details I wish I had known more about when I started my journey through self-publishing. I learned by experiencing many failures. I believe the technical formalities of creating your own book are missing from other products in this space, and they are likely the reason many people never see their work make it to publication.

Most books do not thoroughly explain the E-book creation and publication process, along with the benefits and risks of digital editions. This book lays out all of my experiences and how I choose the platforms available for distribution. Furthermore, it includes a complete tutorial for creating and publishing your own audio version of your book.

I make several assumptions about the reader throughout this entire text. First, I assume you already have an interest in writing your own book. I will not try to convince you to identity a topic, find time to write, and push through the paces required for this task. I will also assume you have the grammatical skills to form sentences, convey a thought, and tell your story. This book will not make you a better writer or explain ways to avoid incorrect verb forms and subject-verb disagreements. This is a technical guide to help you properly create and publish your work.

This entire book was written while executing the steps which I discuss. When I documented formatting of each chapter, I altered my master file in real-time. This ensured that each step is accurate and can be replicated. As I tackled each unique step in the process, I documented my experiences chronologically. As you read along, we experience frustrations and failures together. More importantly, we solve any issues before proceeding to the next task, and all templates are available for download. I believe this provides a unique experience which allows you to make it through the numerous nuances of self-publishing.

While I do not offer much guidance in the world of marketing and self-promotion, I can share some tactics which have worked well for me. Specifically, I explain every detail of publishing your own podcast, including recording audio files and formulation of your podcast feed. Today, over half of my book sales are credited to the listeners of my weekly show.

In summary, this book contains every nugget of wisdom I have gained through my successes and failures within the world of self-publishing. Every technical detail required to publish your print, digital, and audio book is within these chapters. I will help you make every required decision associated with document format, file submission, pricing, distribution, taxes, proofing, personal orders, and online sales. All you need to do is write the content.

CHAPTER ONE
PREPARATION

It is now easier than ever to become a published author. This has resulted in the availability of some amazing niche books which would have never made the cut through traditional publishers. It has also saturated the market with less-than-mediocre content which is not worth the paper on which it is printed. Anyone can self-publish practically any content, as long as it does not violate the copyright of another entity. The entire publishing process can be completed for free, and your work can be made available for online order to the world within 12 hours after submitting your final draft. The striking of keys on your keyboard and clicks from your mouse can be converted into a physical book in the hands of someone in another country within 48 hours. This can all happen without you ever touching a printed copy or facilitating a shipment. We live in amazing times.

The numerous processes required to turn your words into a published title take a lot of work, all of which is explained throughout the chapters of this book. Before we can tackle the details, we should consider some basic preparation. First, you will obviously need a computer. While I have read reports of authors writing, formatting, and publishing E-books completely from an iPad, this is completely unrealistic for printed material. In a moment, I will explain some important hardware considerations which will have a lasting impact on your writing.

Some writers will tell you that the entire self-publishing process can be completed using only free software. This is true, but with many limitations. I will explain my experiences using both premium and free software solutions within this chapter and offer tutorials for both options throughout the rest of the book. Don't worry, you likely already have the hardware requirements met. We just need to tweak some software settings and make sure you are not constantly struggling with software compatibility issues as you proceed through the book.

It is very important to note that technology changes rapidly. Throughout this book, I present extremely detailed tutorials in order to assist with your own self-publishing replication. The hardware and software products referenced here will experience updates, revisions, and other changes. Some of the steps may be slightly different by the time you read this book. Focus on the strategies instead of the details when you detect changes within the tutorials.

Let's start with some basics.

Computer Hardware

You will obviously need a computer. For many, the brand, type, and age may not matter. You can complete the remainder of this book with practically any Windows or Mac computer made within the past ten years. However, your experience may not be optimal, which could make your self-publishing tasks seem like a chore instead of an enjoyable process. Your choice of computer should be based on your own preferences and never from a book written by a stranger. However, I offer a few considerations.

Desktop vs. Laptop: I wrote my first book on a Windows XP Dell desktop. My master copy was always present on this machine, and I could only work on it while sitting in my home office. Today, I insist on a laptop computer which can be easily transported anywhere I may find myself with free time. As I write this sentence, I am in a lobby waiting to give a deposition, which happens to be running two hours behind schedule. Consider the benefits and risk associated with laptop computers. While constant access to your document is convenient, there is increased risk of damage or theft of the device. Offline backups are vital, as explained in a moment.

Operating System: While I prefer a Mac computer over Windows, you should choose the option which is most familiar and comfortable to you. Learning a new operating system while writing a book is not ideal. Stick with what you know, but also understand the benefits and risks of some scenarios. In my experience, Mac operating systems are more stable and require less reboots. If using Windows, I recommend Windows 10 over Windows 7 or 8. When we walk through the proof-ready PDF creation process, it is important to possess an operating system which is up-to-date. Your final product created on a Windows machine should be identical to that made with a Mac, and vice versa. If you happen to be a Linux user, you can absolutely write your book with Linux-compatible software, but you will face issues when exporting PDFs suitable for publishing.

Keyboard: This may seem like a minor consideration, but it is important. Your keyboard should feel comfortable to you. When MacBook laptops switched to a butterfly-style keyboard, many users complained. The new keys were loud and had minimal "travel" which required a light touch to execute a keystroke. There was a learning curve to type without mistakes. If you are buying a new laptop for the purpose of writing your book, test the keyboard at a store first. You may be surprised at how frustrating a new keyboard feel can be.

Overall Stability: This is the most vital consideration. A used laptop with weak battery and failing hard drive can be devastating to your creative process. I don't believe everyone needs to purchase a new machine in order to write a book. However, you should feel confident in your hardware. If there are problems with your screen, keyboard, battery, storage, or internet connection, you will be reminded of these deficiencies at all times. Make sure your computer is fully functioning.

Software Applications

Your computer will need some specific software installed in order to properly complete the self-publishing process. While you could write the entire content within your text editor supplied free by your operating system, you will constantly struggle with formatting. You could use the default PDF creation option within Word or your operating system, but this is inferior to a press-ready document which will appear crisper and generate fewer errors from the publishing services. Popular commercial applications which assist with your creation can become very expensive, often thousands of dollars. Fortunately, there are some maneuvers which will minimize the expense, and often provide an opportunity for free usage. Let's start with the most important software: your word processor.

Word Processor

I am writing this book on my MacBook Pro with Microsoft Word 2019 as my word processor. I paid $150 direct to Microsoft for the entire Office Home & Student suite for my Mac, and it is an offline software solution which does not require an internet connection. The same license could be purchased today on eBay for $80. I believe a full offline version of Word is the best way to go, but the cost can be limiting for some. There are free options, but these have their own issues. Research the following, understand the differences in licensing, and consider my preferred options presented in a moment.

Microsoft Office Online (Free): Microsoft allows anyone to use their core services, such as Word, Excel, and PowerPoint completely free. However, there is a catch. You can only access the programs through a web browser and your documents are stored on Microsoft's servers. There are many reasons this will not work for our needs. First, you will only be able to create a standard PDF export of your final draft which will not play well with book printing services. Next, you are at the mercy of the online service. If your account is suspended, you could lose access to your work. If you do not have internet connectivity, you are stuck. I never recommend this option. For this reason, I also never recommend online providers such as Google Docs.

Microsoft Office 365 ($): This subscription model is the future of software applications as a service. For $69 per year, your license allows you to access all of the Microsoft applications. You can use the online versions or download the full software suite to your computer. I don't like this option for a few reasons. First, you are stuck in a yearly fee in order to continue use of their product. Next, internet connectivity is required. While you can access the offline software without a constant internet connection, Microsoft will lock you out of the applications if you do not allow them occasional access to the internet to verify your license status. Finally, you do not own the software. You are at the mercy of Microsoft allowing you to access the application. Many things can go wrong here, and I am not comfortable with this option.

Microsoft Office 2019 ($): This is the most traditional use of software. You purchase the applications, install them on your machine, enter your license, and that is it. You have permanent use of the software and no need to connect to the internet or pay annual fees. However, there is a catch. While you receive security and feature updates to the software, you will not receive the next major release. When Office 2022 is released, you would need to buy a new copy if you want to upgrade. It is rumored that Office 2022 will be the last version which can be purchased and actually owned for any use desired.

LibreOffice (Free): This productivity suite replicates most of Microsoft Office's features. Word is called Writer, Excel is Calc, and PowerPoint is Impress. The layout of each looks and feels similar to the Microsoft equivalents, but they are not perfect clones. The benefit of this product is that it is completely free. You can download and install it on an unlimited number of machines without any license requirements. As always, there is a catch. Support is limited and searching for solutions to a specific problem with LibreOffice Writer is not near as productive as with Microsoft Word. You can make it work, but expect some frustration.

I highly recommend choosing Microsoft Word 2019 (PC or Mac) as your word processor. At the time of this writing, a license costs $149 direct from Microsoft (Microsoft.com), $117 from Walmart (walmart.com), or $39-$50 from eBay (ebay.com). If choosing eBay, please research the seller and only purchase from those with a solid rating. A license from any legitimate online provider works the same as a code purchased from Microsoft. If cost is truly a factor, LibreOffice Writer can be used. I will explain methods for each of these options as we work through the chapters, but emphasis will always be placed on Word.

Notes Application

I believe the availability of a note-taking application is almost as vital as the word processor required to capture your book. I typically plot each chapter by creating outlines within a program called Standard Notes (standardnotes.org). This application allows you to synchronize your notes from your mobile device to your laptop while being able to access any changes within a web browser on any computer. This is fairly typical of all note applications, but there are a few differences with this specific product. The main feature of this free application is the end-to-end encryption of all content. That means that you are the only person who can access your notes. They are not visible to employees of Standard Notes, or anyone who may compromise their servers. Your content is truly private.

Most people reading this book may not have my level of paranoia. If you have read my previous book *Extreme Privacy*, you know that I can be overly cautious about the online service which I choose. Even if you do not care about privacy, you may like the next unique feature of Standard Notes. The free version allows only plain text entry without any type of markups, formatting, colors, themes, or other bells and whistles. In my opinion, these fancy features can get in the way of creation. Limiting yourself to pure text can be quite freeing. If you find it too plain and do not need to keep your data private from the company which stores it, many people choose Evernote as a flashier alternative. Regardless of your choice, please consider the following.

- **Security:** Make sure your notes application is protected with a secure password. While you may not care if anyone reads your content, you should care if someone is able to access the data. The person could then delete all of your ideas out of spite.

- **Stability:** Choose a provider which saves multiple backups of your data. Standard Notes keeps an offline copy of all backups on your hard drive automatically. It also works in offline mode. This means that you can access your notes without an internet connection. This can become important during long flights or any other areas with restricted internet access. If you rely solely on an online service, you may experience frustration when you cannot access your ideas.

- **Mobile Availability:** I insist on my notes application to be available to me at all times. Downtime while waiting for an appointment or during travel is when I think most about the structure of my current title. I want access on my mobile device which synchronizes to any other places which I have the service installed.

- **Cross-Platform Availability:** The stock Notes application included on Mac machines is a nice product. However, what happens when you need to access the content from a non-Apple machine? I prefer options which function across all platforms including macOS, iOS, Android, Windows, Linux, and web. Both Standard Notes and Evernote fit this criteria.

After you have identified the notes application best for your needs, it is time to start populating ideas, structure, and anything else related to your future book. I prefer to make a separate note for each chapter and sort them chronologically. Figure 1.01 displays my Standard Notes configuration with the Chapter Five note opened. This was captured early within the writing process. The final note for that chapter contained over 100 lines of text.

I do not have much specific advice for note-taking before and during your writing process. That is a very personal and individual decision. However, here are my considerations while planning a new book.

- Document all ideas you have about each chapter in any order as they occur.

- Once you have dumped all of your ideas, reorganize them for each chapter in the order of content, as you want them displayed in the book.

- Keep your notes and outlines brief. Include only the details required in order to begin writing on the topic. Feel free to brainstorm here. I often document potential topics which never make it within the book. That's OK, it is better to have too much than not enough.

I prefer to make sure my notes are completed before writing anything. I want enough content within each chapter's note to convince me I can write the entire chapter including only that information. For this book, I spent 10 hours compiling notes within the chapter outlines. That is less than 10% of the total time spent on the book, but those hours were likely more valuable than the writing. The topics kept me focused on the content and allowed me to write chronologically.

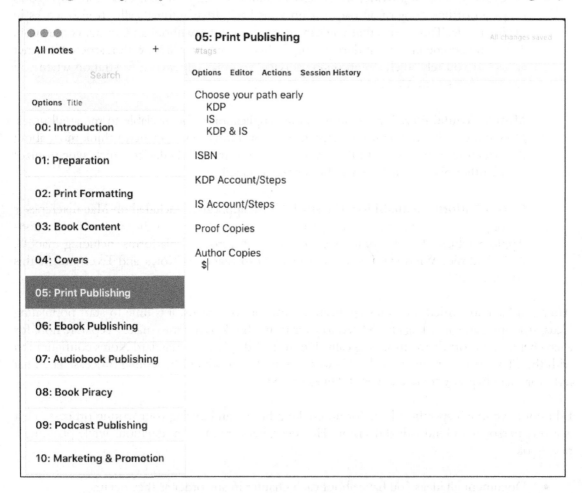

Figure 1.01: Notes usage with Standard Notes.

Adobe Creative Cloud (CC)

This software suite will be vital when we discuss cover design and press-ready PDF creation. Unfortunately, the cost is $600 per year, and you do not truly own the software. That is just the fee to use it. Fortunately, they offer a free unlimited trial for one week. We will take advantage of this later, and only when we are absolutely ready to use it. Because this free trial should not be activated until we need it, I will wait until a later chapter to discuss the usage.

Backup Routine

A solid backup regiment should be established before you write a single word within your new project. Bad things happen. Hard drives crash, files become corrupt, and other mistakes are made. I once saved an empty Word document over my existing master file of a book I was finishing. If you ever experience the act of deleting your only copy of your words, you will never forget the feeling of your stomach collapsing which soon follows. We should always save numerous copies of our work on multiple data storage sources. I will share my strategy.

The first document I created for this book was titled "This Book Was Self-Published.01.docx". After a few days, I saved a new copy titled "This Book Was Self-Published.02.docx". Any time I made substantial changes to the master document, I saved a new copy with a new number at the end. A typical book I am writing may have dozens of files, each a bit unique. My previous book, **Extreme Privacy**, has a folder which contains the following files (name and size).

Extreme.Privacy.01.docx	487kb
Extreme.Privacy.02.docx	513kb
Extreme.Privacy.03.docx	845kb
Extreme.Privacy.04.docx	1.1mb
Extreme.Privacy.05.docx	1.1mb
Extreme.Privacy.06.docx	1.3mb
Extreme.Privacy.07.docx	1.5mb
Extreme.Privacy.08.docx	1.5mb
Extreme.Privacy.09.docx	1.5mb
Extreme.Privacy.10.docx	1.7mb
Extreme.Privacy.Final.docx	1.7mb

As you can see, each file grows in size as I add new content. In a perfect world, you will never need a file which is not the most current. However, disaster can strike at any time. While I was working with the fourth file listed above, I suffered a computer crash which required a forced reboot. I found my file to be corrupted. Since the changes to that file from the previous were minimal, I was able to open the third file and simply re-write the latest content. Imagine if my only copy had corrupted. I would have had to start over. Multiple files can also be beneficial if you ever want to revisit a specific section before it was modified. I often re-read previous versions of paragraphs which were later heavily modified. This strategy preserves your writing as you go, and the file sizes are minimal.

Next, we should worry about storage failure. If you keep all of your versions of your documents on the internal hard drive of your laptop, you are risking loss of all of your work. Hard drives crash without warning. I have lost several during my lifetime. This is why a backup is vital. My routine is as follows.

I keep a folder on my laptop titled "Books". Inside this folder are subfolders of each of my books, such as "This Book Was Self-Published" for this title. Inside each book's subfolder are the versions of documents which I previously described. I keep an exact copy of the "Books" folder on an external USB drive which is usually with me at all times. Any time I save my document, I save a copy on the USB drive. Once a week, I copy my "Books" folder to a second USB drive which never leaves my home. This way, I have three copies of all of my files at all times. If my laptop bag is stolen while I am out, I lost my master file on the laptop and the secondary backup file on the primary USB drive. However, I have that third copy at home. Is this overkill? I don't think so. Consider the following event which I witnessed in 2019.

My former boss called me in a panic. He had been writing a crime novel and was near the end of the project. When he opened the Word document, it was blank. Something had corrupted the content, and all data was lost. I asked if he had any backups, which he did. However, they were spread all over his computers and USB drives. They all had the exact same file name and various file sizes. The dates of the files were sporadic. He had been updating numerous files instead of a single "latest" document. He had no choice but to grab the largest file, begin reading from the start, and try to find missing sections within the various files spread across his devices. This is why I always recommend files with chronological names which can easily be understood. These should be stored as a "master" copy (on your computer), a "secondary" backup (on a USB drive), and an "emergency" backup (on a USB drive) which never leaves your home. If disaster strikes, attempt to recover the most recent files in the same order of devices.

The most important lesson here is to test your file creation and backup strategy. Make sure you understand how your files are titled, stored, and duplicated. Pretend your most recent file has become corrupt. Replicate what you would do to salvage the situation and make sure your data works as intended during this test. There is a scene in the movie *Royal Tenenbaums* where a father forces his young children to conduct a fire drill in case of an emergency. Think of that moment in regard to your document files. If you have confidence in your backup and recovery strategies, you will be prepared if something bad happens. If you write enough books, your preparedness will be tested at some point.

Hopefully you now have a stable computer, appropriate word processor, synchronized notes application, and tested backup strategy. We still have a long way to go before we are ready to write our masterpiece. Please trust me when I say that all of this preparation will pay off. Once you start writing, none of the traditional roadblocks will be able to stifle your creativity.

Next, you should consider your title and author name.

Title Selection

In the previous demonstrations, I already knew the title of my pending book. Do you already know yours? Let's dive into a discussion about titles. Most self-publishing advice leans toward creating your title AFTER the manuscript is finished. I never liked that, and I have always known the title before I typed a single word. If I have enough notes and an outline, I should have some ideas for titles. Knowing the title helps keep me within the scope of my vision for the book. I offer the following considerations for your own title selection.

Keep it short: Long titles often get truncated on social network posts and sales pages. Short titles are easier to type and say. They also appear easier to read on digital devices with small screens. I prefer titles five words or less. If you need more words to provide context, consider a subtitle.

Make it easy to remember: The best publicity for your book is word of mouth. Make sure your title is memorable and easy for your readers to advertise.

Make it descriptive: Your title should include keywords which describe the most important idea in your story or topic.

Provide only a preview: Your title should not give all of the content away. Leaving some mystery may motivate purchases.

Consider the cover: Your title and cover should pair together nicely. If your cover has no connection to your title, it may confuse people. Later, I explain the choices and creation of my own cover based on the title.

Make it easy to enunciate: If your title is difficult to pronounce, it may cause confusion. It may also prevent people from recommending it. You don't want a mention on TV or radio to be incorrect due to a title which is hard to get out. I have heard numerous people mispronounce my book *Open Source Intelligence Techniques* during keynote introductions and conversations. I wish I had taken more time to create something easier to say. Simplify your title while you can.

Consider the future: You are going to see the name of your book constantly. Make sure it is something that you will not regret later. I typically avoid rhymes and catchy sayings in my titles, as the novelty wears off quickly.

Consider a subtitle: I always use subtitles with my non-fiction books. It gives me a little more room to explain the content. Subtitles can also increase the likelihood of your book being found online through search terms. I don't believe a subtitle should be an extension of the title, but it should be a separate thought. With this book, the title is fairly self-explanatory. The subtitle, *A Technical Guide*, tells the potential reader that this book gets technical and guides through the process.

Pseudonyms

I have one final preparation consideration. What name will you use? Most authors proudly place their true name on the cover of their book and move forward. If you already have an online presence or want to enhance your career, this makes the most sense. However, if you plan to publish anything controversial, you might consider a pseudonym. This may only apply to a small number of readers, but take a moment to weigh the options.

I have published under both my real name and an alias. A book such as this work is a fairly safe topic, so I used my real name. If I were writing a political exposé, hacking handbook, or anything which may upset people, I would likely use a pseudonym. This would not prevent a court order to Amazon which would still identify you, but may stop crazy people from finding your home address and causing trouble.

Some question the legalities of pseudonyms, or fictitious names. I assure you it is completely legal with the following exceptions.

- You cannot register for your Amazon account under a pseudonym.

- You cannot complete the required tax reporting documents under a pseudonym.

- You cannot accept payments under a pseudonym.

All of this will be explained later, but I want to make sure to cover the rules here first. The public-facing portion of your book can be completely protected by your pseudonym, but anything official on the backend must be your true identity. If you have genuine concerns about sharing your real name with Amazon and other publishers, there are options. You could create an LLC, obtain an Employee Identification Number (EIN) from the IRS for the LLC, open a banking account under the LLC's EIN, and provide only the LLC details to the publishers. I have done this, and it is not overly difficult. However, it exceeds the scope of this book.

In the final chapter, I explain individual, sole proprietorship, and LLC formation options for consideration of your project. Because of this and many other factors, I ask you to finish the entire book before replicating my actions. There are many considerations which all work together in harmony to properly execute your own project. During many of the steps there is no do over, and you should already know the path which you will choose when you get to it. This is especially true if you want to properly hide behind a pseudonym.

OK, paranoia aside, it is almost time to start building the structure of your book. First, consider the following checklist. I present a checklist at the end of each chapter in order to summarize the topics and also ensure that you are considering all details before jumping into the next section.

Preparation Checklist

- Obtain a stable Mac or Windows computer.

- Apply all system updates.

- Obtain a comfortable keyboard.

- Install an appropriate word processing application.

- Install an appropriate notes application for outlines.

- Create a proper file storage and backup routine.

- Test the files and backups.

- Select the title and subtitle of your book.

- Choose your displayed author name.

CHAPTER TWO
PRINT FORMATTING

Some authors may begin writing within a blank document without consideration for formatting. You can always copy and paste the raw text into a properly configured document later. However, I do not recommend this strategy. I prefer to build my book template before writing. This helps me determine page views, the page length of chapters, and the overall vibe of the project. Since I write non-fiction, this also allows me to skip around as desired. I can navigate directly to a later chapter, modify the content, and easily find my way back to the previous chapter. This should make more sense by the end of this chapter, especially if you follow along.

Figure 2.01 displays my view of the previous paragraph. I am using Microsoft Word, and I have the "Ruler" view enabled by selecting the ruler checkbox under the "View" menu. It is vital to keep this option enabled. It allows you to make sure that your page alignment is appropriate for the left or right page which is being edited. If you look at the margins in Figure 2.01, you will see that the right margin is narrower than the left. This is because this is a right-facing page which needs a larger margin near the spine of the book. Don't worry, I will provide a template which does the work for you, and this is just an early demonstration in order to explain the importance of a properly-formatted document.

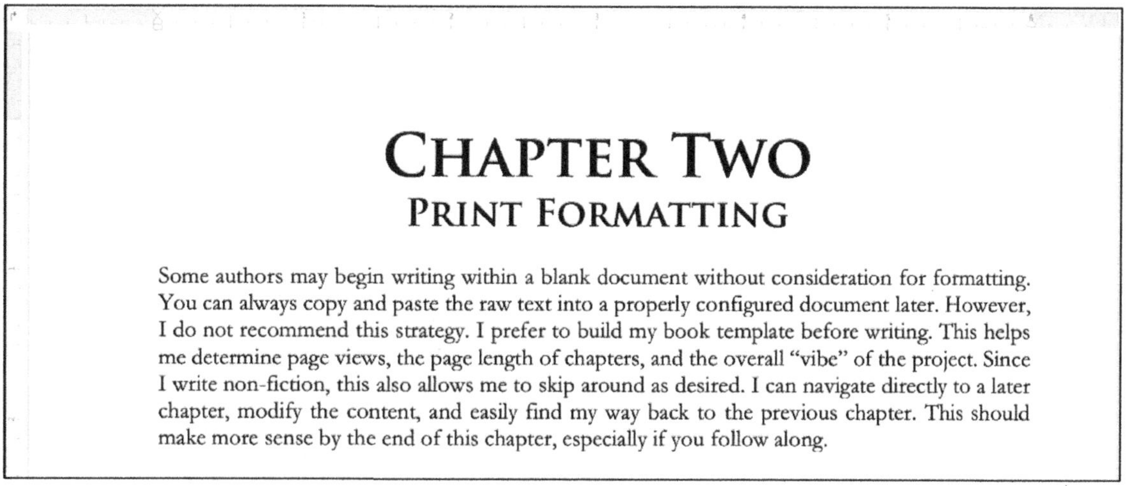

CHAPTER TWO
PRINT FORMATTING

Some authors may begin writing within a blank document without consideration for formatting. You can always copy and paste the raw text into a properly configured document later. However, I do not recommend this strategy. I prefer to build my book template before writing. This helps me determine page views, the page length of chapters, and the overall "vibe" of the project. Since I write non-fiction, this also allows me to skip around as desired. I can navigate directly to a later chapter, modify the content, and easily find my way back to the previous chapter. This should make more sense by the end of this chapter, especially if you follow along.

Figure 2.01: The view of this page within Microsoft Word with the ruler visible.

Print Book Dimensions

The first decision you should make about your book is the "trim size" of the final product. This is the width and height of your printed book as measured by any single page. The most common trim size for paperbacks in the U.S. is 6" x 9" (15.24 x 22.86 cm). This may work well for fiction novels, but it is not optimal for my needs. Almost all of my books were created as 7.5" x 9.25" (19.05 x 23.5 cm) products. I find this to be the perfect size for technical books, especially if images and screen captures will be presented. If you are reading the print version of this work, you are holding a 7.5" x 9.25" book. Before choosing this size, I visited a local bookstore and measured the dimensions of books which felt right to me.

Selecting the size of your book before writing has several benefits. Choosing a standard size now will prevent many headaches later. All self-publishing services demand specific trim sizes and reject any submissions which do not conform to these requirements. Amazon demands your book to be one of the following trim sizes.

5" x 8"	(127 x 203 mm)	7.44" x 9.69"	(189 x 246 mm)
5.06" x 7.81"	(129 x 198 mm)	7.5" x 9.25"	(191 x 235 mm)
5.25" x 8"	(133 x 203 mm)	8" x 10"	(203 x 254 mm)
5.5" x 8.5"	(140 x 216 mm)	8.25" x 6"	(210 x 152 mm)
6" x 9"	(152 x 229 mm)	8.25" x 8.25"	(210 x 210 mm)
6.14" x 9.21"	(156 x 234 mm)	8.27" x 11.69"	(211 x 297 mm)
6.69" x 9.61"	(170 x 244 mm)	8.5" x 8.5"	(216 x 216 mm)
7" x 10"	(178 x 254 mm)	8.5" x 11"	(216 x 280 mm)

IngramSpark, which will be discussed later, demands one of the following trim sizes.

4" x 6"	(102 x 154 mm)	6.625" x 10.25"	(168 x 260 mm)
4" x 7"	(102 x 178 mm)	6.69" x 9.61"	(170 x 244 mm)
4.25" x 7"	(108 X 178 mm)	7" x 10"	(178 x 254 mm)
4.37" x 7"	(111 x 178 mm)	7.44" x 9.69"	(189 x 246 mm)
4.72" x 7.48"	(120 x 190 mm)	7.5" x 9.25"	(191 x 235 mm)
5" x 7"	(127 x 178 mm)	8" x 8"	(203 x 203 mm)
5" x 8"	(127 x 203 mm)	8" x 10"	(203 x 254 mm)
5.06" x 7.81"	(129 x 198 mm)	8" x 10.88"	(203 x 276 mm)
5.25" x 8"	(133 x 203 mm)	8.25" x 10.75"	(210 x 273 mm)
5.5" x 8.25"	(140 x 210 mm)	8.25" x 11"	(210 x 279 mm)
5.5" x 8.5"	(140 x 216 mm)	8.268" x 11.693"	(210 x 297mm)
5.83" x 8.27"	(148 x 210 mm)	8.5" x 8.5"	(216 x 216 mm)
6" x 9"	(152 x 229 mm)	8.5" x 9"	(216 x 229 mm)
6.14" x 9.21"	(156 x 234 mm)	8.5" x 11"	(216 x 280 mm)
6.5" x 6.5"	(165 x 165 mm)		

Since we want a trim size which is compatible with both services, we must select from the following options.

5" x 8"	(127 x 203 mm)	7" x 10"	(178 x 254 mm)
5.06" x 7.81"	(129 x 198 mm)	7.44" x 9.69"	(189 x 246 mm)
5.25" x 8"	(133 x 203 mm)	7.5" x 9.25"	(191 x 235 mm)
5.5" x 8.5"	(140 x 216 mm)	8" x 10"	(203 x 254 mm)
6" x 9"	(152 x 229 mm)	8.5" x 8.5"	(216 x 216 mm)
6.14" x 9.21"	(156 x 234 mm)	8.5" x 11"	(216 x 280 mm)
6.69" x 9.61"	(170 x 244 mm)		

Note that Amazon and most other publishers charge a printing fee per page, regardless of size. A 200-page 5" x 8" book will cost you the same in printing fees as a 200-page 8.5" x 11" title. This is one reason I prefer larger dimensions for my books. They are simply a better deal. If I had published this book in a smaller size, it would have required more pages, and cost you more money. After you have chosen your desired trim size, you can download a document template created specifically for those dimensions. This is the biggest benefit of beginning with this step. The templates contain proper section breaks, opposing page margins, and many other formatting configurations which will save time and headaches later. Navigate to the following website and click the download option titled "Download (Templates with sample content)" to your computer.

https://kdp.amazon.com/en_US/help/topic/G201834230

If this link has changed since the writing of this book, conduct a search of "KDP paperback templates" through your chosen search engine in order to identify the new page. In case these templates disappear, I have archived a copy at the following link.

https://inteltechniques.com/selfpublish

This file is compressed and the content must be extracted before the templates can be used. Windows, Linux, and Mac users should be able to simply double-click the file and "extract" all of the content to your desired storage location. Once you have the content extracted, you are presented numerous language folders which each contain document templates. I chose the "English" folder then selected the "7.5 x 9.25 in.docx" file. I right-clicked on the file, selected "Copy", and pasted a duplicate copy of this file directly onto my Desktop (right-click then "Paste"). I then renamed the new copy of the file on my Desktop to the title of the book, similar to This Book Was Self-Published.docx. This became my first master file.

This template is a great start, but it is far from perfect. It is the standard Amazon format for self-publishing. You could get away with making no changes and simply adding your content, but I believe this is a mistake. I see several books which have this exact layout, which is an obvious sign that the author used a stock template. We can make things much better while adding some personalization to your book. Let's start with some general layout tweaks.

Fonts, Paragraphs, and Spacing

Once you open your appropriate document template which was previously downloaded, take a look around. Scroll through and notice the different sections devoted to various introductions and chapters. The overall look is fairly generic, but we will make many changes. As you may have already noticed, the structure of your template is quite different than this book. However, I assure you I started with the same template you are using. First, let's clean up the fonts.

The default chapter content font inside the templates is Garamond 11 point. While I like this font, I do not like the size. I find it a bit too small. Additionally, I have found some empty lines within the templates to default to Calibri 11 point. I want to eliminate any hidden font changes so I will change the font and size to the entire book at once. I conducted the following steps within the document, which applies to both Microsoft Word and Libre Writer.

- Press "ctrl" and "a" ("command" and "a" on Mac) on the keyboard to select all text.

- In Microsoft Word, click "Home" in the title bar.

- In Libre Writer, click the font drop-down menu.

- Change the font to your desired option (I chose Garamond).

- Change the size to your desired option (I chose 11.5).

Your entire content should now all be the exact same font. This is not the desired option for our final product, but we have more changes to make. This action eliminated undesired fonts from causing conflict within empty areas of the text. This will eliminate great frustration as you write.

If you are using Libre Writer, you likely noticed the absence of Garamond and many other popular fonts. While the program may display Garamond in the font selection menu, it is not present within the application. Since Garamond is not a free font, you would need to download something similar or choose another font. The closest replica I have found is EB Garamond available for download at https://www.fontsquirrel.com/fonts/eb-garamond. I conducted the following steps, which should only be considered if using Libre Writer instead of Microsoft Word.

- Navigate to https://www.fontsquirrel.com/fonts/eb-garamond.

- Click the "Download OTF" button and save the zip file.

- Double-click the downloaded zip file to view the contents.

- Double-click each desired font such as EBGaramond12-Regular.

- When prompted, choose the option to install the chosen font.

- Open your document within Libre Writer.

- Press "ctrl" and "a" ("command" and "a" on Mac) on the keyboard to select all text.

- Change the font to your desired option (I chose EB Garamond 12).

- Change the size to your desired option (I chose 11.5).

Regardless of your chosen word processor software, you should now have an entire document with a single font and size of text. Next, we need to modify the spacing. The template files from Amazon include various line spacing settings which can cause a lot of confusion when trying to make each paragraph look identical to the others. Some sections of the template include wide line formatting while others have narrow configurations. I prefer to wipe out all of the anomalies with the following steps.

- Press "ctrl" and "a" ("command" and "a" on Mac) on the keyboard to select all text.

- If using Microsoft Word, right-click any text and choose "Paragraph".

- If using Libre Writer, right-click any text, highlight "Paragraph", then choose "Paragraph".

- In the "Spacing" section, enter "0" in both the "Before" and "After" fields.

- If using Word, make sure "Line Spacing" is set to "Single".

Your entire document is now free of any undesired line spacing. Striking enter or return on your keyboard will move your cursor to the next line without fear of spacing issues which may make the text appear different than within previous paragraphs. This will eliminate frustration later when a paragraph would have otherwise refused to split properly between pages.

Your document template is already configured for proper spine margins. Take a look at your pages within the template and notice that the margins are unique for every other page. The second page within the template is aligned to appear on the left while the third page is set for the right. The margin closest to the spine of the book is larger than the margin closest to the edge, as explained at the beginning of the chapter.

I recommend keeping these settings. In my experience, tweaking these margins can cause bleed issues which result in a rejection from the publisher. The margins present within the templates are approved for use with all self-publishing printers and create an even flow to the book. After we are finished writing and have created a proof-ready PDF, I will explain how to visually check the margins throughout the entire book within a proper full-screen view.

If you plan to document any websites, email addresses, or other internet-related content, I encourage you to disable hyperlinking. By default, if you type the address of a website, such as www.inteltechniques.com, Word creates an underlined hyperlink in blue color. You can see this within the previous sentence. This can cause undesired print issues. Since I will be referencing many websites, I decided to disable the feature with the following steps.

- In Word, find "Options" or "Preferences" inside the file menu.

- Click the "AutoCorrect" option and click "Autoformat as you type".

- Disable "Internet and network paths with hyperlinks".

In the previous chapter, I introduced a checklist feature. The official method for adding checkboxes within Microsoft Word is to enable the "Developer" tab and insert them manually. I find these entries to present formatting issues, so I inserted standard bullet points instead. Many online blogs encourage writers to insert checkboxes by clicking the "Home" tab, then the drop-down menu next to the "Bullets" button, and defining a new checkbox bullet from the "Wingdings 2" Unicode image set. Figure 2.02 displays a typical selection window with the checkbox option circled. Do not use any Unicode characters within your self-published book! At the time of this writing, KDP cannot process PDF documents which contain Unicode characters such as checkboxes from unsupported fonts. I include this image only to help you identify areas of Word to avoid.

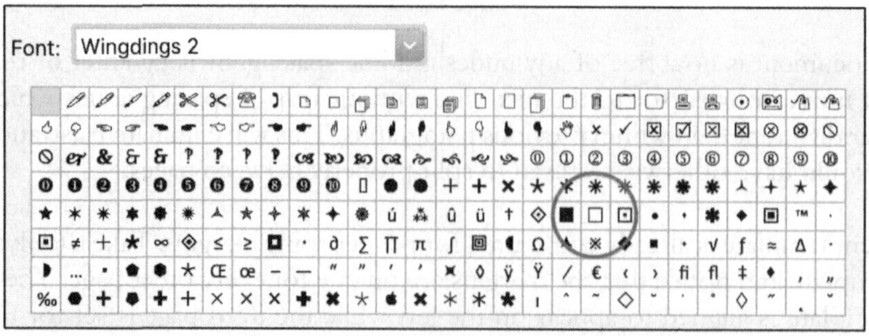

Figure 2.02: Unicode characters, which should always be avoided.

Chapter Headings

Since we have changed the font of our entire text, the chapter titles may appear smaller than desired and in a generic display format. The heading of the first chapter of your template should now appear as follows by default.

```
1 CHAPTER NAME
```

I prefer each chapter to display a dual-line announcement including the chapter number and title. The example below is identical to the first chapter within this book. It displays the chapter number in Trajan Pro (28 point) with the chapter title below it in Trajan Pro (18 point). I like Trajan Pro because it is clean, powerful, and all uppercase with a slightly higher first letter.

CHAPTER ONE
PREPARATION

The default templates include six empty lines in order to provide extra space between the top of the page and the chapter title. I prefer no space there and the chapter heading to appear at the top of the page. In general, I do not like too much empty space as I find it to be a waste of valuable real estate within any book.

If you are using Libre Writer and find Trajan Pro to be missing, it can be downloaded from the website at https://www.wfonts.com/font/trajan-pro and installed using the previous directions. This font should already be included within Microsoft Word.

Obviously, I am sharing my own preferences for fonts. The options are endless, and you should choose fonts which deliver your text as you desire. On the guidance of various self-published authors, I have experimented with Baskerville, Caslon, Garamond, Jensen, Minion, Palatino, Sabon, and Utopia. Consider writing a paragraph and testing each of these fonts throughout the entire text. Websites which display a single word in a specific font never give a real-world view. You can always change the font later, but each change will alter all of your spacing. I highly recommend settling on your font before writing.

Headers and Footers

One of my favorite comedians, Brian Regan, delivers a bit about book headers. He questions the need for the title of a book to be present at the top of each page. Do people actually forget what they are reading, only to be saved by the presence of the title on each page? I do not like any headers in my books, so I eliminate them completely. Double-click the header in your template which displays "BOOK TITLE", highlight the text, and delete it. This should remove the header throughout the entire book. Double-clicking on the body of the page text will take you out of the header edit screen. You can also use this instruction to add the name of your book or modify the header in any other way.

Unlike headers, I believe footers are essential. Your template already displays a centered page number at the bottom of every page. My preference is to move the page number of left-facing pages to the left and the right-facing pages to the right. I also prefer the left-facing pages to include the chapter number while right-facing pages display the chapter title. Let's tackle all of this with the following steps, starting with instructions for Microsoft Word.

- Double-click the footer within the first chapter of your template.

- In the "Header & Footer" tab, enable the "Different Odd & Even Pages" option.

- In the "Header & Footer" tab, disable the "Different First Page" option.

- Select the page number within the right-facing page (wide margin on left).

- In the "Home" tab, click the "Align Right" button to move the number to the far right.

- Select the page number within the left-facing page (wide margin on right).

- In the "Home" tab, click the "Align Left" button to move the number to the far left.

- In the right-facing page, add the chapter title prior to the page number.

- In the left-facing page, add the chapter number after the page number.

- If desired, change the font (I chose Garamond 11 point).

- If desired, change the text highlighting (I chose a bold page number).

- Repeat for each chapter.

If you are reading the print version of this book, take a look at the footers of these two pages. The left page has the page number followed by chapter number on the left while the right page has the chapter title followed by page number on the right. I find this more visually appealing than a centered number. It also allows the reader to quickly flip through a book and find a desired chapter. Figure 2.03 displays the footers of two pages for those reading the electronic version of this book. Figure 2.04 displays a closer view of a left page while Figure 2.05 presents the right. Replicating this behavior within Libre Writer is possible, but sometimes difficult. I took the following steps within Writer to modify my template.

- Choose "View" then "Styles" to open the "Styles" menu on the right.

- Expand the "Footer" option.

- Right-click "Footer Left" and select "Modify".

- Change "Next Style" to "Footer Right" and click "OK".

- Right-click "Footer Right" and select "Modify".

- Change "Next Style" to "Footer Left" and click "OK".

- Click inside the first page in your document.

- Double-click "Right Page" in the list of page styles in the "Styles" window.

- Scroll through your template and make the desired footer changes as explained previously.

In theory, this should allow you to replicate the footer settings previously explained using Microsoft Word. However, I often encounter problems defining right and left pages within Libre Writer. When necessary, I have to double-click "Right Page" or "Left Page" in the list of page styles in the "Styles" window after selecting the footer inside every page. This can be very time consuming. However, once your template is configured correctly, it should hold the settings for all additional pages added to your template. This is another reason I believe a properly-configured template should be the first step, and Microsoft Word is always preferred over Libre Writer. Word consistently handles footers better. I could not imagine modifying hundreds of footers after a book is complete. Footers were a constant headache with my first few books. Since I now insist on a properly-configured template before I start writing, the problems are minimal.

On occasion, I also find a template which gives me problems with footer modification within Microsoft Word. While writing this chapter and applying my edits in real-time, I encountered a common issue. When I changed the left footer of Chapter Two, it also changed the left footer of

Chapter One. When I updated the footer to read "Chapter Two" within this chapter, it changed the left footer of Chapter One to display the same text. The solution to this issue is to conduct the following within Microsoft Word or Libre Writer.

- Create the desired footer within the first chapter.

- Double-click the footer area within the next chapter.

- In the "Header & Footer" tab, deselect the "Link to Previous" button.

- Modify the footer in the next chapter as desired.

- Repeat as needed.

Footers can be tricky. Notice that I always begin a new chapter within the print version of this book as a right-facing page. This ensures that the new section possesses a footer which is right-justified and displays the chapter title. This is my preference, but you can modify this to fit your own needs. I have spent countless hours trying to identify the culprit when a footer is on the wrong side or the alignment is off. If you struggle with this, the default centered page number is absolutely acceptable, especially within fictional novels.

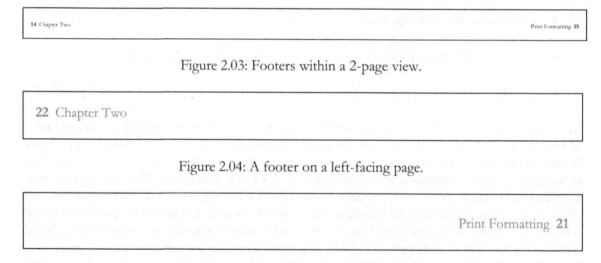

Figure 2.03: Footers within a 2-page view.

Figure 2.04: A footer on a left-facing page.

Figure 2.05: A footer on a right-facing page.

Title Page

Your current title page at the beginning of your template is fairly boring. Instead of a centered title, I prefer a title at the top, the subtitle directly below it, and the author at the bottom. In this book, my title is in Trajan Pro (28 point), while the subtitle and author is in Trajan Pro (16 point). Figure 2.06 displays a screen capture of my title page.

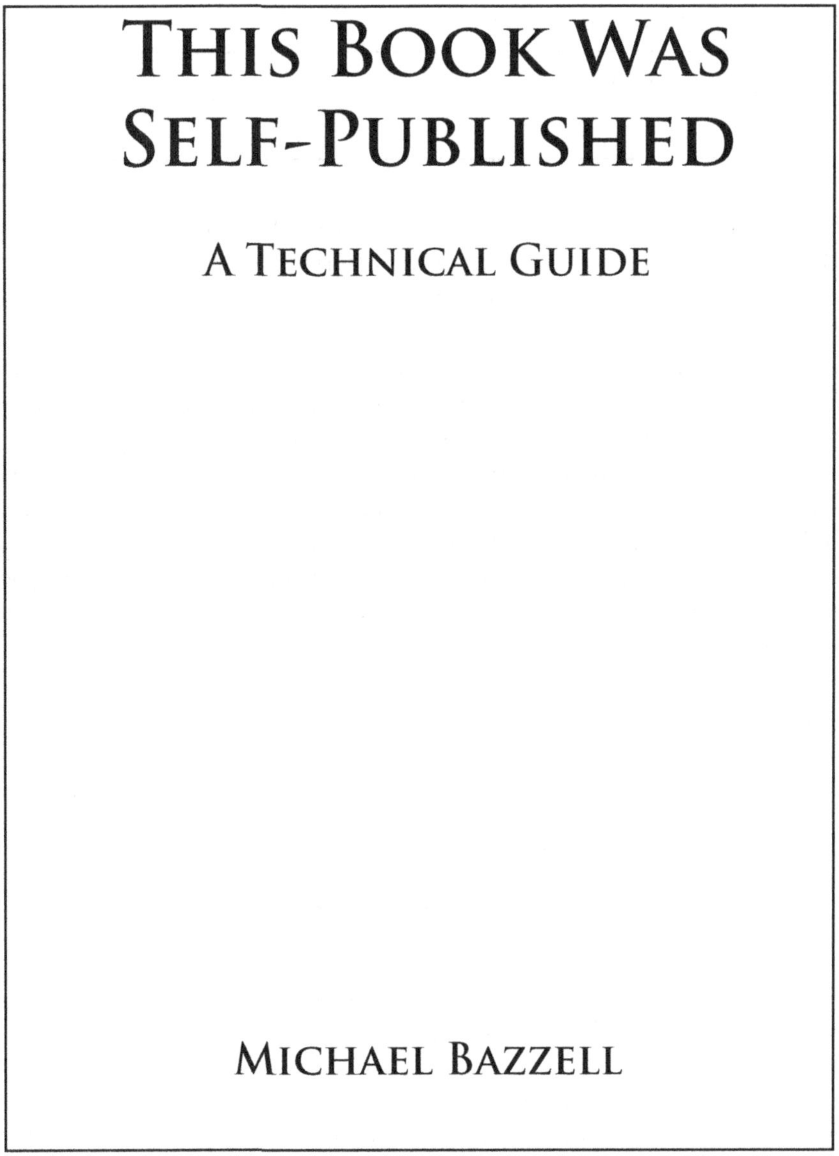

THIS BOOK WAS SELF-PUBLISHED

A TECHNICAL GUIDE

MICHAEL BAZZELL

Figure 2.06: The title page of this book.

Formalities Page

This second page of a self-published book is often overlooked. This is your opportunity to provide any formalities such as the full title, copyright details, restrictions, and legal considerations. The following replicates the page from this book, but includes comments about each section.

Title: This is self-explanatory, but you should have your full title in default font on this page. I prefer the subtitle below the title, as seen below.

> **This Book Was Self-Published:**
> A Technical Guide

Copyright: The topic of copyright protection is often surrounded by inaccuracies and misleading sales pitches. I hope to clear up some confusion by offering four levels of copyright protection, most of which are free. Let's start with the basics.

- **Automatic Copyright:** Technically, you do not need to take any action in order to possess a minimal layer of copyright protection. Copyright law in the U.S. is governed by the Copyright Act of 1976. This Act prevents the unauthorized copying of a work of authorship. However, only the copying of the work is prohibited, and anyone may copy the ideas contained within a work. For example, a copyright would cover the written text within this book, but the topic of self-publishing itself is not covered. Therefore, one could not legally copy the exact text presented here, but anyone could use the methods discussed to replicate other similar work. The moment you publish your book, you have U.S. copyright protection.

- **Declared Copyright:** It is not necessary to place a copyright notice in your book for it to be protected by copyright law. However, I believe we should all make our intentions of claiming copyright transparent. This book included the following line on the second page.

> Copyright © 2020 by Michael Bazzell

- **Registered Copyright:** Copyright can be registered at the Copyright Office in the Library of Congress, but there is no legal requirement for this while maintaining protections. The current fee to electronically file your copyright registration for a single book is $45. The first step is to complete Form TX, which can be found online at the official copyright website at https://www.copyright.gov/forms/formtx.pdf. If creating an E-book without a print version, you can submit your work online. If publishing a printed book, you are required to send a physical "best copy" as directed within the application process. The benefit of this strategy is that you have a government entity which can offer evidence in the event you are engaged in civil litigation surrounding the ownership of your work. I find this overkill for most self-published writers. Therefore, I did not register this book. The registration process can take several months.

- **Evidence of Copyright:** This is often referred to as the "Poor man's copyright". An author may place the book in a sealed envelope and mail it to himself, maintaining the seal. If ever questioned in court, this sealed package with a date stamp could save the day. This method is not recognized by law and offers no more protection than any of the previous strategies. I believe you are wasting your time and postage when doing this. Better evidence includes detailed notes during the writing process, digital copies of your work, screen captures of the final publishing steps, and online evidence at Amazon and other retailers.

ISBN: Once you know your International Standard Book Number (ISBN) for your title, which is explained later, you should include it on the second page. This further enforces copyright protection. Mine appears as follows.

ISBN: 978-0-578-74438-4

Acknowledgement: This is a dedicated area to acknowledge the work of others who assisted your creation. I typically use this area to list any editors. My acknowledgements are typically short, since I do most of the work myself. Yours may have dozens of people. Mine is as follows.

Project Editors: Ashley Martin, M.S. Williams, D. Sapp

Restrictions: This is your official notice prohibiting specific actions from being performed against the content of your work. I use this to declare that no one can replicate the content of this book and distribute it outside of any official channels determined by me. This is mostly targeted at people who upload the content to websites which offer free illegal downloads of books. This will be explained more later. This is only a formality, but may give you some power if you decide to challenge a website which has copied your material. Mine reads as follows.

Publication Date: This is supporting evidence for your copyright claim. Mine reads as follows.

First Published: September 2020

General Liability: This is a legal catch-all which may prevent someone from successfully suing you due to your content. It is your chance to declare that you are not responsible for any bad things which occur to a reader due to your words. Mine reads as follows.

> The information in this book is distributed on an "As Is" basis, without warranty. The author has taken great care in preparation of this book, but assumes no responsibility for errors or omissions. No liability is assumed for incidental or consequential damages in connection with or arising out of the use of the information or programs contained herein.

Trademark Liability: If you include trademarked terms within your writing, you may want to declare the usage as "editorial". As an example, I mention Amazon a lot throughout this book. I am not trying to claim any official affiliation with Amazon, nor displaying any trademark images as my own. The following explains my usage so they do not sue me.

> Rather than use a trademark symbol with every occurrence of a trademarked name, this book uses the names only in an editorial fashion and to the benefit of the trademark owner, with no intention of infringement of the trademark.

Unique Disclosures: If you include any text which does not conform to traditional grammar rules, you may want to explain this ahead of the content. Most writers will not need this. I always include the following paragraph about my usage of quotation marks in order to avoid the constant complaints about my writing from the grammar police.

> Due to the use of quotation marks to identify specific text to be used as search queries and data entry, the author has chosen to display the British rule of punctuation outside of quotes. This ensures that the quoted content is accurate for replication. To maintain consistency, this format is continued throughout the entire book.

Technology Liability: The final piece I include is a summary of the technical editing which was conducted and a disclaimer about technology changes. Mine appears as follows.

> The technology referenced in this book was edited and verified by a professional team for accuracy. Exact tutorials in reference to websites, software, and hardware configurations change rapidly. All tutorials in this book were confirmed accurate as of August 1, 2020. Readers may find slight discrepancies within the methods as technology changes.

Let's have a reality check here. None of these actions will prevent someone from stealing your content, suing you, or complaining about the content. These are all formalities which are proactively providing a small layer of protection. You cannot go back in time and change these words after someone is causing you troubles, so choose your wording carefully.

Dedication Page

I do not include dedication pages due to my privacy concerns for me and my family. However, most writers display some sort of "thank you" to someone at the beginning of a book. This could be a spouse which put up with your countless hours isolated in your office, children who inspired some of your writing, or anyone else who had an otherwise hidden impact on you. I am not the expert on dedication pages, but I offer a few considerations.

Priority: If you list numerous people in this page, some may question the order of their placement on the list. Did you mention your brother before your spouse? This can cause unrest when the book comes out.

Publicity: Anyone who reads your book will see this page. While it may seem like a personal note to a loved one, it is in every copy printed. Make sure that anything you say here is appropriate for permanent archiving.

Permission: I encourage you to obtain permission from anyone which you want to list in the dedication of your book. Some people may not want their name in print while others may simply not want it in YOUR book.

Brevity: In contrast to the acknowledgments section mentioned previously, the dedication should be brief. You should not mention everyone who contributed to the book's creation, unless you specifically want to repeat these names.

Finally, don't spend much time on the perfect dedication page. While everyone will see it, no one but the people you mention will remember it. If you doubt this, think of your favorite book dedication. Chances are you do not have one. Many people display something light, funny, or creative, such as the following true examples.

To the nine publishers who turned me down

For my parents, who never once to my knowledge tried to kill me

To those who inspired it and will not read it

This book is for my parents, who tried

Contents Pages

The contents page provided within the Amazon interior templates is minimal to say the least. It will get the job done, but I prefer more style and page coverage. This may be one of the most important sections from a marketing perspective. The Amazon "Look Inside" feature, which allows potential buyers to preview partial content of your book, almost always includes the entire table of contents. Many people quickly browse through this section in order to decide if your book will provide enough value to justify the purchase, especially with non-fiction titles. I encourage you to include every main topic covered within your work in order to maximize sales potential.

The following is an excerpt of my contents page which displays the topics within this chapter. I used Garamond (12 point) bold uppercase for the chapter and Garamond (12 point) standard for each topic and page number. I also applied a continuous dotted line to connect each topic to the corresponding page. If desired, you could copy this text from the digital template which I offer in just a moment. This page will be completed after you write the content of your book, but having a template ready now can be beneficial.

I believe this is much more visually pleasing than the standard offering from Amazon, which appears as the following.

1	Chapter Name	1
2	Chapter Name	3
3	Chapter Name	6
4	Chapter Name	9
5	Chapter Name	11
6	Chapter Name	17

Author Page

The Amazon interior template files place the author page at the end of the book, which I find odd. I believe your author page should be presented before any chapters in order to identify your credentials or experiences, which the reader should know. For non-fiction, it should clearly state any details which make you an authority on the subject. Fiction titles can be more forgiving of this, but should still include interests or history which gives your voice credibility. I share two of my author pages below. The first is from this book while the second is from *Extreme Privacy*. Note that the first option focused on the topic of books while the second provides more detail about my work history as it applies to privacy. Author pages should be brief and less than one-half of a page. This is not a resume or pitch for employment. Tell the reader enough to trust you without boring them with details which have no relevance to your authority on the subject.

Michael Bazzell investigated computer crimes on behalf of the government for over 20 years. As a side-hustle, he has self-published eighteen books since 2012. After leaving government work, he served as the technical advisor for the first season of the television hacker drama *Mr. Robot*. His books *Open Source Intelligence Techniques* and *Extreme Privacy* have become training manuals for intelligence gathering and privacy hardening within both government and private sector communities. Both titles continue to sell thousands of copies annually. He now hosts the weekly *Privacy, Security, and OSINT Show*, and assists individual clients in achieving ultimate privacy, both proactively and as a response to an undesired situation.

Michael Bazzell investigated computer crimes on behalf of the government for over 20 years. During the majority of that time, he was assigned to the FBI's Cyber Crimes Task Force where he focused on various online investigations and open source intelligence (OSINT) collection. As an investigator and sworn federal officer through the U.S. Marshals Service, he was involved in numerous major criminal investigations including online child solicitation, child abduction, kidnapping, cold-case homicide, terrorist threats, and advanced computer intrusions. He has trained thousands of individuals in the use of his investigative techniques and privacy control strategies.

After leaving government work, he served as the technical advisor for the first season of the television hacker drama *Mr. Robot*. His books *Open Source Intelligence Techniques* and *Extreme Privacy* are used by several government agencies as mandatory training manuals for intelligence gathering and privacy hardening. He now hosts the weekly *Privacy, Security, and OSINT Show*, and assists individual clients in achieving ultimate privacy, both proactively and as a response to an undesired situation.

Paragraph Indention Formatting

You may have noticed that each of my paragraphs in the print version of this book do not include indentation, but possess a blank line between them. This is fairly standard with non-fiction books. Fiction titles typically include an indent without a blank line. I highly recommend that you decide on your format now and stick with it. If you are reading the E-book, you will notice that each paragraph is indented without a line space. This is typical of E-books and is the default conversion option with EPUB and Kindle Create, as explained later. The source of the E-book content was the document form the print version, but we are getting ahead of ourselves.

Bullet Spacing

In my other books, I do not include an empty line break in between each bullet item. Those books are fairly dense with information and already approaching 600 pages. Because of that, I cram in the bulleted items. I deviated from that strategy in this title. I believe it allows and encourages readers of the print version to insert their own notes and experiences as techniques are explained. Either option is acceptable. However, you should replicate whichever option you choose throughout the entire book for consistency.

Custom Template

You may be replicating the steps as we go and find yourself experiencing more problems than those described within this chapter. I understand your frustration. I have screamed at my monitor, punched my keyboard, and promised to never self-publish another book on numerous occasions. The nuances of both Microsoft Word and Libre Writer seem to creep into your workload at the worst times. My offering to you is this exact template in digital form. It can be downloaded at the following website.

https://inteltechniques.com/selfpublish

This template was created for this specific trim size, but could still be used in other sizes. As one example, assume you are having trouble getting your footers to align properly with left and right pages. Open this custom template, copy a desired footer, and paste it into your own document. The font, spacing, and configuration should carry forward to your own document. You could also copy and paste chapter headings, chapter introductions, or anything else which presents complications. If you plan to release a 7.5" x 9.25" book, you could simply modify the text within my master and avoid many problems.

Print Formatting Checklist

- Select your trim size.

- Download the appropriate template.

- Select and apply your fonts.

- Choose and apply all spacing.

- Configure hyperlinks and checkboxes.

- Configure chapter headings.

- Eliminate page headers if desired.

- Create page footers as desired.

- Modify your title page.

- Create your formalities page(s).

- Consider a dedication page.

- Create your contents template page.

- Create an author page.

- Choose your desired indentation and spacing strategy.

- Download a custom template for comparison.

CHAPTER THREE
BOOK CONTENT

Now that you have your template ready, chapters outlined, fonts placed, footers configured, and formalities complete, it is time to write the content. Until this point, we have focused on the technical specifications which can be replicated by following simple tutorials. Ideally, that was the easy part. The pressure to write the book itself is completely on you. I am not an expert on the creative writing process and have no tricks to motivate you to write your masterpiece. However, I can share some experiences, both positive and negative, which I have encountered throughout my previous books. After this chapter, we continue down the path of self-publishing technicalities.

Determine your reasons for writing a book: I find it quite difficult to write daily if I do not know why I am writing. I need a specific goal and vision of the final product. For this book, I had two goals. First, I selfishly wanted documentation of my entire self-publishing protocols. Every time I write a book, I encounter the same obstacles throughout the entire process. I promise myself that I will keep better notes when I discover the best workarounds, but I never do. This book provides as much benefit for me as it may to you. Next, I simply wanted to share my experiences in the hopes it would help others battling the same issues. I recently published the second edition of *Extreme Privacy*, and the eighth edition of *Open Source Intelligence Techniques* is not due until next year. This was a great time to commit to the project.

Why do you want to publish a book? Some may desire credibility as an authority on a subject. Others may want to see their name on Amazon. Many just want some extra income. Until you understand your own motivation for writing a book, I suspect you will encounter much frustration and procrastination while you attempt to complete the process.

Overcome excuses which prevent you from writing a book: It is easy to find a reason to avoid writing. A decade ago, I spent three years convincing myself that I did not have the time, authority, or ability to finish anything which would seem valuable to others. Let's dissect each of these.

- **Time:** My first contract with a traditional publisher outlined explicit deadlines. Each chapter was due on a specific date, which made my stomach hurt. I was worried I would miss deadlines, which would cause me to rush and create mediocre content. Self-publishing removes this stress. There are no deadlines or demands. This can be done around your own schedule. While I encourage you to write every day, this is not mandatory. However, I believe if you have time to find something to watch on Netflix, you have time to write.

- **Authority:** You may suffer from imposter syndrome. This is a psychological pattern in which one doubts one's accomplishments and has a persistent internalized fear of being exposed as a fraud. I see it a lot in the cybersecurity community. I have experienced this myself. In fact, I am hesitant to publish this book as I write this sentence. I am a college dropout who always struggled in school and made horrible grades. I probably have no business telling others how to write their own book. However, notice that I am still writing. You do not need to know everything about the topic of your book. As long as there is a knowledge gap between you and the reader, and you have something unique to offer, you can push through any insecurities. Do not place unnecessary pressure on yourself to be the expert. If you are passionate or knowledgeable about a topic, then you are qualified to write a book about it.

- **Ability:** Some may believe they simply cannot convey their thoughts in a cohesive manner throughout an entire book. Others may worry about grammar complications. I worry that my chronological way of thinking is not transferred to the reader in a way which is easy to digest. I encourage you to eliminate this thinking and simply write. I also have my own "blog test". Before I begin writing a book, I create a series of blog posts about the topic. I do not always publish them, but I ask a few close friends to read them and tell me if they understand the topics and instruction. Be sure to find friends who are not afraid to provide constructive criticism.

Possess a title and outline first: This may not be your preference, but it is mandatory for me. I insist on knowing the title of my book before I write a single word. I want to always know the title which represents the content. It keeps me focused on the overall idea for the book. I also spend weeks curating my outline of chapters and content. Before I begin writing, I already have the order of topics for each chapter. This helps me write faster without considering the placement of my ideas. I will present more thoughts on titles later.

Write chronologically whenever possible: Most writers find it easiest to write from beginning to end. This helps eliminate redundant writing or inaccurate references. If you write a bit in chapter ten and then write about a similar topic in chapter four, you are likely to leave out details presented in the later chapter which could be vital for the reader in the earlier chapter. While it is acceptable to tell the reader that more explanation will be provided in a later chapter, it is not ideal to present the exact same material twice because you need to repeat yourself in order to make sense. I struggled with this during the audiobook and podcasting chapters, which are unique, but similar.

Accept imperfection: Your first draft will have problems. You will misspell words, commit grave grammar mistakes, write run-on sentences, and fail to present your thoughts appropriately. Do not try to be perfect as you write. I typically never look back. My goal for a first draft is to document my ideas and structure. I do not edit as I write. Repairing spelling and grammar can interfere with the creative process. There is always time to fix things later.

Identify writer's block: I believe every author faces writer's block on occasion. This is typically due to the fear of others' opinions of your work. I have found the following to help me.

- **Revisit the outline:** If you have a solid outline of ideas, identify the topics which have not been completed within the section where you are stuck. This often generates new ideas.

- **Re-read the previous pages:** Go back a few pages and restart your reading. Get back into the flow of the content leading to the block. This can often help you get back into the groove.

- **Change something physical:** I often relocate to a different area of my house. When I am in the office and struggling for words, I take the laptop into a different room. Sometimes, relocating outdoors can have a huge impact. I have also found that standing versus sitting can alter my flow of ideas.

- **Skip:** When necessary, skip ahead to the next section, topic, or chapter. This can often refresh your thoughts and allow you to return to the blocked topic with new ideas.

- **Escape:** If desperate, take a break. I have had many days where nothing I did helped me get the thoughts and words into the computer. I usually just walk away from it, sometimes for a couple of days. Remember, there is no deadline pressure with a self-published book. Forced writing often leads to mediocre content. Don't settle for inferior words. Come back when you feel ready to conquer the project.

Finish the first draft: I feel like I am cheating when I transition to this section. A lot of work must go into your book before it becomes a first draft. I do not want to minimize your efforts by jumping to this so quickly, but I cannot help you generate the content of your work. Finishing the first draft is a huge accomplishment. You possess the rough version of your book. Now, it needs some help.

Spelling and grammar review: Before you re-read your work, you should consider a review of your content by your word processing software. This is never a replacement for true editing, but it may catch some obvious mistakes. The spellcheck features of Microsoft Word and Libre Writer are very similar, but the grammar review options within Word are much superior. Let's walk through both options.

- In Microsoft Word, click "Review" within the upper menu, then "Spelling & Grammar". Before conducting a review, make sure your language is set to the appropriate option. Mine is set to "English (United States)". Click the "Options" button and make sure the settings are as desired. I typically do not change anything. Allow the software to identify potential problems and make manual changes as necessary.

- In LibreOffice Writer, click "Tools" within the upper menu, then "Spelling". Before conducting a review, make sure your language is set to the appropriate option. Mine is set to "English (USA)". Click the "Options" button and make sure the settings are as desired. I typically do not change anything there. Allow the software to identify potential problems and make manual changes as necessary.

Become the first editor: After you have allowed your word processing software to locate any obvious mistakes, it is time to read the entire work while looking for errors or modifications. I typically re-write sentences or entire paragraphs during this read. I am looking for areas which present confusion or poor wording. I estimate that I change 20% of the book during this first edit. I am also looking for any errors. I try to modify anything before an outside editor looks at my work. When complete, this is now the second draft. However, I also leave a few grammatical errors in place. This is to test my outside editors to make sure they are reading the work. I typically leave something extremely obvious, spelling errors such as "to" instead of "too", plus something a bit harder to notice. Of the three examples which were left in my first draft of this book, my editor found all three, which was comforting. However, I left one of them in. Will you find it? The first person to email me the error at error@inteltechniques.com will receive a special gift.

Find two additional editors: Regardless of your confidence that your first draft is perfect, you need outside editors. Asking friends and relatives to read your book while looking for errors is great, but not enough. At least one of these editors should be a professional. This could be a full-time editor or teacher with experience in grammar. It should not be a relative, friend, or co-worker. Ideally, it should be someone who does not know you personally and is not afraid to offend you. You want honest and aggressive feedback. My editorial process is as follows.

First, I have a friend or family member with a strong background in education or grammar read the second draft, identifying any problems. I then apply any feedback they provided, which creates the third draft. I re-read the entire book which now includes my own edits and the "friendly" editor feedback. This creates the fourth draft, which is finally ready for outside review. I hire an editor to review this draft to reply with feedback and corrections. The response should be substantial. My hired editor typically locates problems which escaped me and my friendly editor. After I apply the appropriate changes to my master document, I now possess the fifth draft. I typically walk away from it for a few days, and then read the entire book one last time in order to make sure I am happy with the content. This creates the sixth and final draft.

Hiring professional editors: You must first decide on the type of editing you require. There are typically three types of editing, and I explain each.

Developmental: This is the most involved editing. Your editor looks at the big picture and may recommend some drastic structural changes. This will be the rawest feedback you will receive, and opinions on the topic of your writing style may clash quickly.

Copyediting: This type of editing looks at spelling, grammar, and the overall flow of sentences, paragraphs, and chapters. This is beneficial if you have struggled with documenting your thoughts cohesively.

Proofreading: This is the most standard editing option which looks only for obvious spelling and grammar errors. I typically seek this type of service since I feel confident in the overall flow of my content (you may disagree with that statement by now).

Once you understand your needs, it is time to find the perfect match. There are numerous online services which will pair you up with an editor. I have experience with Guru, Upwork, Reedsy, and Fiverr. Of these, I have had the best success with Guru (guru.com). The rates for professionals on Upwork and Reedsy seemed highest while some amateurs on Fiverr were lowest. I found the rates on Guru to be the fairest and the reviews reliable. Do your own research and use the service most appropriate for you.

These sites allow you to post a description of your needs and wait for the offers to roll in. I do not like this strategy. In my experience, you will get bombarded with people who are desperate and never contacted directly for work within their chosen platforms. Instead, I encourage you to read reviews, study pricing, and contact editors which seem to match your needs. I typically send an email such as the following to many potential editors.

I found your profile on [insert site]. I am seeking an editor to review the final draft of my book about [insert general topic]. It contains [insert number] words and [insert number] pages at [insert trim size]. I am not seeking developmental assistance at this time, and looking only to focus on obvious spelling and grammar issues. Can you please answer the following?

- What is your fee for this manuscript and service?

- Do you have previous experience with books about [insert topic]?

- Can you describe your last editing project and the types of changes you proposed?

You will likely get two types of responses. The majority will be canned messages which do not acknowledge your specific questions. The desired responses should provide the details you requested. Focus on those first. If your editor cannot read through your message and create an acceptable response, clearly acknowledging any details requested, they should not be trusted as the final editor of any book.

I always prefer a project price instead of an hourly rate. You should know what you are getting into and everyone should agree on the package price. Some standard industry payments for basic proofreading cost between $1.50 and $3.50 per page, or $0.01 and $0.03 per word. Copyediting and developmental work can be higher. I estimate this book would cost between $500 and $750 for a professional proofreader. Consider the fees from the proposals, but don't make cost the single determining factor in whom you hire. The rapport with the person during your initial interactions often identifies the ease or pains which may follow.

I want to stress the importance of limiting the number of editors for your book. If you hand out a dozen copies to everyone in your inner circle, you will very likely receive conflicting opinions on everything from topics of chapters to the proper usage of the word whom. Also, I never recommend distributing copies of your book to more than one person at a time. During the editing of my second privacy book, I gave copies to three people in Microsoft Word format. All three tracked their changes and returned the files. After I applied an edit of one file, I would see a contradiction of the same edit in the next. By the third, I could no longer recall my initial verbiage or the first editor's recommendation. This creates a confusing mess. I always recommend applying one person's edits which you find valuable, then send a new draft to the next editor. Make sure that all editors track the changes in Word in order to quickly see the differences from your draft.

Spacing review: After I know the content is grammatically correct, I go through the book looking for various issues. I want a natural view of the book, with left-facing pages displayed on the left and right-facing pages on the right. Your Word document or PDF file likely does not do this, so we need to make a few modifications. First, save your Word file as a PDF using the methods presented in the next chapter. Then, complete the following.

- Open your final PDF within your trial of Adobe Acrobat Pro (explained later).

- In the menu, click "View", "Page Display", then "Two-Page View".

- In the menu, click "View", "Page Display", then "Show Cover Page In Two-Page View".

- In the menu, click "View" and enable "Read Mode".

You should now see a single first right-facing page. Striking the down arrow on your keyboard should navigate through the book with each page presented on the appropriate side. Now that you have a proper view, you should scrutinize each page for the following issues.

- **Footer page numbers:** I ensure that each left page has a footer page number and description which is left-justified, and then repeat the process for the right pages. I also look to make sure the footers are generally in the same position on each page.

- **Chapter headings:** I prefer each chapter to begin on a right-facing page. This presents consistency and helps keep page footers aligned properly. This natural view should make it easier to make sure your chapters begin as desired.

- **Paragraph spacing:** Since this is a non-fiction book, I ensure that there are no indents within paragraphs and that a blank line exists between paragraphs.

- **Paragraph justification:** If you chose to "justify" your text so that it creates a block view, instead of sentences ending at different positions, you should verify this is consistent throughout the book. I often see paragraphs lose formatting, which requires simple modifications.

- **Page margins:** I ensure that the first sentence of every page is truly at the top of the pages. Sometimes, a blank line can creep into the beginning of a page, which is undesired.

- **Page splitting:** I make sure that the final paragraph of every page is split appropriately. If there is only one sentence at the bottom of a page, I push it down to join the remaining paragraph on the next page.

Create an Index: Once you know that your overall structure and pages are locked into place, you can create an Index for the back of the book. I typically create a spreadsheet with two columns. The first column contains every topic presented throughout the book while the second column contains the page numbers possessing the content. I then alphabetize the list and merge the two columns. This list is copied and pasted into the final page of the book, with a three-column layout. If you have downloaded the template for this book, you can play with my Index and place it into your own work if desired.

Update the table of contents: I previously explained my desired formatting for my contents page. You should now update this page with the desired topics and page numbers. I typically create a PDF of my current draft, open it on the left side of my screen, and open the active Word document on the right side of the screen. This allows me to scroll through the PDF while modifying the data within the Word document.

Create backups: This is an appropriate time to remind you about the importance of backups. If necessary, revisit the backup strategies previously presented. You should not proceed unless you are confident you possess multiple files of your current work which are easily retrievable.

Embedded Images

The next section of this chapter is fairly heavy in images, so we should have a discussion about embedded graphics within a document. Microsoft Word possesses a tool to insert screen captures, or partial captures, directly into your document, but I do not recommend it. It generates a PNG image file which is highly compressed and smaller than the original. Let's examine the evidence.

As I wrote this paragraph, I used the embedded Microsoft Word tool to grab a cropped screen capture of the words presented above. I then replicated the capture using the default tool within my Mac computer. The capture created by Word was 432 x 60 pixels while the Mac capture was 800 x 84 pixels. The second option was much clearer, larger, and more legible, even though it captured the exact same area of content. My recommendations are as follows.

Mac: On a Mac computer, my routine is as follows. While viewing image content which I want to include in my book, I press command-shift-4 on the keyboard. This converts my cursor into a crosshair. I can now click and drag the crosshair to select a custom box around the desired image content. This saves a full-resolution PNG image file to my Desktop. I then use the "Insert" > "Pictures" > "Picture from File" option within Word to insert the capture I just created. Double-clicking on the image opens the "Format Picture" menu on the right which presents tools to crop and resize your capture.

Windows: In Microsoft Windows operating systems, you can use their embedded screen capture tool. Press the Windows key-shift-s on the keyboard. The screen will dim and the mouse pointer will change. You can drag to select a portion of the screen to capture. The screenshot will be copied to the clipboard, which you can paste directly into Word or Writer. Alternatively, you can use the Snipping Tool application within Windows. First, open the Snipping Tool from the Start menu. In the "Mode" option, choose the type of screenshot shape you want, such as a rectangle. Click "New", and your screen will freeze. You can then use the mouse to create the screenshot. The screenshot will then appear in the Snipping Tool window and can be saved for import into Word.

Expect your images to look worse in print than they do in your digital document. Even Kindle versions possess a maximum of 300 ppi (pixels per inch) and appear grainy. Always insert images which are clear and large. Never insert a screen capture of your entire desktop if you are using a high resolution. The reader will not be able to tell which portion you are trying to emphasize. If necessary, print a few pages which possess images and see how they look on paper. This is best done with a black and white laser printer.

Compressed Images

Various versions of Microsoft Word handle image compression in different ways. If you have inserted beautiful high-resolution photos into your work, Word may be compressing them to lower quality versions in order to save storage space. This may not be noticeable to the print or E-book readers since they are being shown versions which are less than 300 ppi. However, a poorly compressed image which is then recompressed a second time can look awful. My recommendation is to preserve the full resolution of all images throughout the draft and PDF export process. This gives you the best possible display now, and later mandatory compression can be completed by the publishers when required. Here are my considerations for Microsoft Word.

Windows: When you save and close your documents within Word for Windows, it automatically compresses your images in order to reduce file size. This can be a huge hindrance. Before you embed images into your file, consider disabling this feature with the following steps.

- Within Word, click "File" then "Options".

- In the "Options" box, click "Advanced".

- Within "Image Size and Quality", select the current document.

- Disable the "Discard editing data" option.

- Enable the "Do not compress images in file" option.

- Save the document and re-open to continue editing.

Mac: By default, Mac versions of Word do not compress images unless you force it to. Clicking "File" in the menu and then "Reduce File Size" generates a new compression menu. This allows you to select the level of compressions and provides an option to delete the cropped areas of images. This removes all of the undesired areas within cropped images which can substantially decrease the file size. I only recommend this utility if your file size exceeds a publisher's limits.

It is always best to possess the highest quality files as possible in your master copies. You can always compress images later, but you can never decompress them once your changes have been saved. By disabling the compression feature, you maintain the ability to re-crop images later if desired. Your full image is available to you, and only the cropped version is visible until you select the crop option within Word. If your file size exceeds a publisher's limits, begin compression at the highest resolution and try again. Continue to lower the resolution one step at a time until you meet the file size requirements. Since most publishers offer generous file size limitations, I have never had to compress any of my documents.

Press-Ready Interior PDF

This may be one of the most important sections of this entire book. Many self-published authors simply create a PDF file within their word processor (Windows) or through a print option within their operating system (Mac). This is a mistake. These options do not properly embed your fonts into the file, nor conform to industry standards for professional printing. I once accidentally submitted a standard PDF for printing, and the proof copy had a light grey text with a few incorrect fonts. When we create a PDF of our work, we want it to print exactly as it was intended and as we see it. In order to do this, we must possess some expensive software, which we will obtain for free with a one-week trial. **Please finish this entire chapter before you replicate my steps.** There are important considerations at the end. First, let's understand the differences in PDF formats.

Every publisher encourages users to submit a PDF file of their final interior work. While Amazon can accept a Microsoft Word document format, you will likely receive many warnings about format conversion when submitting during the print version process. A standard PDF may appear exactly the way you desire, but there could be many hidden problems. A specific version of PDF known as "PDF/X-1a:2001" solves these issues. This is a protocol which is quite old (2001), but remains an industry standard. A PDF/X-1a file conforms to the following rules.

- All fonts are embedded into the file.

- All color data is grayscale, CMYK, or named spot colors.

- Files do not contain music, movies, or non-printable annotations.

- Files do not contain forms or JavaScript code.

- Encryption is not present.

- Transfer curves are not present.

While "PDF/X-1a:2003" (a slightly newer version) could likely be used without any issues, there are some printers which prefer the legacy 2001 option. In order to please any potential printing press software, I prefer to stick with the 2001 setting. The PDF in this format should ensure clearer text and images than a standard PDF. Now, let's configure our system to have the ability to create these superior PDF files.

First, we must download the Adobe Creative Cloud Desktop Application from their website at https://www.adobe.com/creativecloud/desktop-app.html. When you click the "Download" button, you will likely be forwarded to a login screen for active Adobe users. Instead, click the "Create an account" link to become a new trial user. You will be asked to enter your email address. I highly recommend using a junk or "forwarding" account such as AnonAddy or Simple Login (these are great privacy protections which I talk about in **Extreme Privacy**). Adobe will bombard you with spam, so provide an appropriate email address. Next, enter the name you wish to provide Adobe and any date of birth which makes you an adult. I never provide my real date of birth. Choose a unique password and make sure you document it for later use.

You should be prompted to download the installation file. When complete, launch the file and click any install option present. In some scenarios, you may be asked to log in to the service through your browser with the password you previously chose. The Creative Cloud Installer should run through some standard installation routines. This does not install any application which we need; it only installs the Adobe framework which allows us to install any applications later.

During the installation process, you will likely receive an email from Adobe asking you to confirm the email account which you provided. This is not mandatory, but you may get locked out of your trial if you do not follow the instructions. During this tutorial, I confirmed the email account.

Once the Creative Cloud Desktop is installed and launched, you should see the option to "Try" or "Buy" various applications. Figure 3.01 displays an example of this application menu. Locate the Acrobat DC program and click the "Try" button. This will install Adobe Acrobat Pro to your computer, which will allow us to create the PDF document which we need. You will have only one week of usage of this program unless you want to pay for a monthly or yearly subscription. We will also use this trial to create our cover in the next chapter.

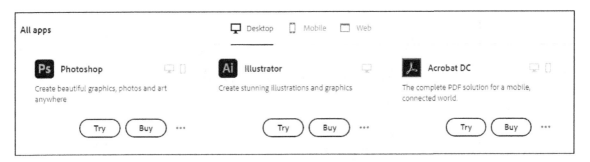

Figure 3.01: The Adobe Creative Cloud Desktop application.

After your Acrobat DC trial is installed, we want to set the default PDF creation option. In your Windows menu or Mac Applications folder, launch the Adobe Distiller program. Change the "Default Settings" option to "PDF/X-1a:2001". Figure 3.02 displays this setting for the Windows operating system. This will ensure that the software is configured to create the most appropriate file for our needs by default. Some combinations of word processor and operating system do not let you choose the conversion settings during each export, so the default settings could save us from future frustration.

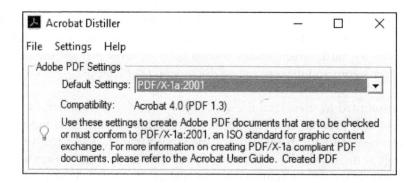

Figure 3.02: The Acrobat Distiller default settings configuration menu.

Next, close Acrobat and launch Microsoft Word. You should see some new options in the menu bar. If you are using Microsoft Word for Windows, open your document and click the "Acrobat" option in the menu. Next, click the "Preferences" button. Change the "Conversion Settings" option to "PDF/X-1a:2001" and click "OK". When your final document is ready for PDF generation, click the "Create PDF" button within the Acrobat tab inside Word. Clicking this opens a dialogue asking for the location of your saved PDF file. Clicking "Save" generates a press-ready PDF. Figure 3.03 presents this option.

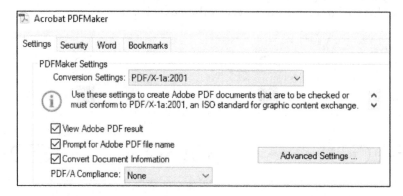

Figure 3.03: The Acrobat configuration menu launched from Microsoft Word (Windows).

If you are using Microsoft Word for Mac, things work a bit differently. While your document is open, click the print button. In the lower left, change the "PDF" dropdown menu to "Save as Adobe PDF". In the print dialogue box, choose "PDF/X-1a:2001", make sure the "After PDF Creation" option is set to "Launch nothing", and click "Continue". When prompted, choose a file name and storage location for your PDF. Figure 3.04 presents this option.

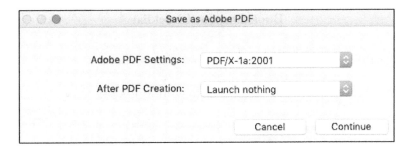

Figure 3.04: The Adobe PDF generation window (Mac).

If you are using LibreOffice Writer, open your document and click the "Print" option. Make sure the "Printer" option is set to "Adobe PDF", and click the "Properties" button. Similar to the previous Windows instructions, change the "Default Settings" option to "PDF/X-1a:2001" and click "OK". Click "OK" in the print dialogue box and select a file name and location for your document. Figure 3.05 displays the print menu with Adobe option.

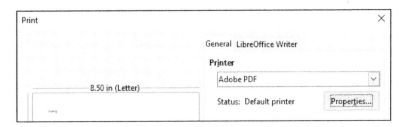

Figure 3.05: A print dialogue box within LibreOffice Writer.

Regardless of the word processing software or operating system, you should always check your final PDF to ensure it is the proper format. Launch the Adobe Acrobat DC program, open your document with the "File" and "Open" menu options, and open the "Properties" option within the "File" menu. Click the "Custom" tab and ensure that the version is "PDF/X-1a:2001".

Hopefully you now have your final PDF file which will be used to submit your work. Remember that you only have one week from the execution of your trial to export the document without any cost. Timing is critical, especially if you will be using Adobe software to design your cover. Note that the free trial of each program starts when you install the specific application, and not when you install other Adobe programs. As an example, you could start a free trial of Photoshop after your trial of Acrobat has expired.

I promise that the effort to export a proper PDF file for your interior will create a more professional book and easier reading experience. Next, it is time to consider your book cover.

Book Content Checklist

- Determine your reasons to write a book.

- Overcome excuses which prevent you from writing a book.

- Confirm your title and outline.

- Write the bulk of your content.

- Disable image compression.

- Conduct a spelling and grammar review.

- Execute the first edit (you).

- Execute the second edit (friend).

- Execute the third edit (professional).

- Conduct final spacing review.

- Conduct final footer review.

- Complete the table of contents.

- Create an index.

- Export press-ready PDF.

CHAPTER FOUR
COVERS

People absolutely *will* judge your book by its cover. My first self-published book's cover contained a solid grey background, white title in the upper-right corner, and white descriptive text on the back. It had no images, textures, or interesting fonts. It also had no one who liked the cover, including myself. At the time, I simply wanted to write a technical book full of tutorials related to online investigations. I knew nothing about cover design, and really didn't care to learn. That was one of many mistakes I made during that initial attempt at self-publishing. Today, I insist on a cover with a bit more pizzazz. Before going any further, I must disclose that I am not an expert on book covers. I have never received any education related to design. I don't always understand the differences between fonts and typefaces. You may not want to take design advice from me. However, I can share my experiences creating covers and walk you through all of the technicalities of the creation process. Publishers are very strict about formatting, bleed, barcodes, embedded fonts, and size. This chapter will explain all of these issues and provide easy solutions.

Instead of writing a chapter telling you how to choose and create a cover for your book, I will explain every detailed step I took to create the cover for this title. These instructions can be applied toward your own work. My goal is to explain my process which should translate into benefiting your own experience. This chapter is focused more on software tutorials instead of graphic design.

As I write this sentence, I do not have any cover created. In fact, I don't really know what I want it to look like. I envision something bright with light text, and possibly a graphic which somehow relates to the idea of self-publishing. Outside of that, I have no idea what I will create. Together, as I write this chapter, we will witness the results in real time. I plan to possess a final cover by the end of this chapter, preferably within a few hours. Let's begin.

Similar to interior content, the first step with cover design is to know the size of your book. Unlike the interior, we must also know the total number of pages before we can download a cover design template. This book has dimensions of 7.5" x 9.25" with a total page count of 214 pages after completion. Note that this is the number of pages as reported by your word processor, and not the last page number within the footer of your content. Once you know your total size, navigate to the official Amazon cover design template page at https://kdp.amazon.com/en_US/cover-templates and enter the details. Provide your desired paper color, which is typically white, and download the file to your computer.

The downloaded file will be in zip format, so you will need to extract the contents to your computer. Most operating systems allow you to double-click the file, and choose a location to which you can extract the content. In my situation, the zip file generated by Amazon was titled "BookCover7_5x9_25_BW_220.zip". If I had entered a page count of 221, the file would have been titled "BookCover7_5x9_25_BW_230.zip". This is because Amazon generates a unique file for every ten pages of content and not every specific page count.

Inside the zip file is a folder with two files. I only want the PDF, which for me was titled "7.5x9.25_BW_220.pdf". I saved this file within the same area where I keep my master interior document. At this point, I possess a folder titled "This Book Was Self-Published". Inside of it are folders titled "Interior", "Cover", and "Templates". My master document is in the "Interior" folder, and all templates from Amazon are in the "Templates" folder. The "Cover" folder will be used for any graphics and final cover documents.

I prefer to conduct all cover design within Adobe Photoshop. Fortunately, you are allowed a free one-week trial, similar to the Adobe Acrobat application within the previous chapter. Launch the Creative Cloud Desktop application as you did previously. Click the option to "Try" Photoshop and allow the program to install. Launch Photoshop and accept the offer for a free trial. The clock is ticking, so only do this when you are ready to create your cover.

Within Photoshop, open the PDF cover template previously downloaded. Mine is titled "7.5x9.25_BW_220.pdf". Photoshop should prompt you with an "Import" dialogue. Simply click "OK" and you should see the template file. Figure 4.01 displays mine.

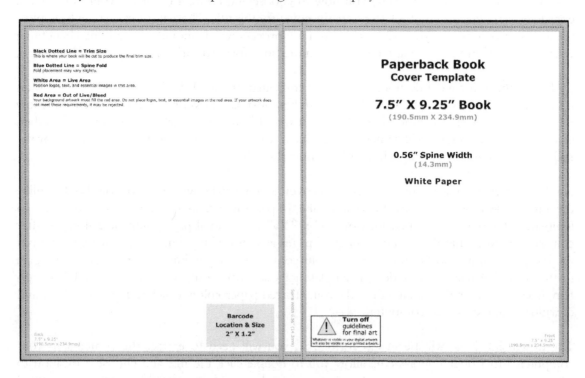

Figure 4.01: The cover design template provided by Amazon.

This template identifies the cover, back, and spine of our book. It is vital to stay within these boundaries if we want a proper cover which is accepted by the publisher. Next, I want to consider the image or artwork I want on the cover. While you may be tempted to search across the internet and copy an image you like, this is a huge mistake. Most online images possess strict licensing for usage. If you blindly copy an image and place it on your book, you could be targeted for a copyright lawsuit. This is extremely common when people unknowingly use images licensed by Getty on their covers. I know someone who received a very threatening letter from them with an offer to settle out of court for $4,000. Don't get caught in that trap.

Instead, let's focus on royalty-free images. I prefer to start at Pixabay (https://pixabay.com). This free service shares copyright-free images and videos. All contents are released under the Pixabay license, which makes them safe to use without asking for permission or giving credit to the artist, even for commercial purposes. It is one of the only safe places to download truly free images.

I began my search with terms such as book, pencil, notebook, and other keywords which could present an image which felt appropriate for my book. I considered a typewriter on the cover, but that really made no sense. A typewriter is never used throughout the process, which made an image of it misleading. A computer seemed more relevant to this book than a typewriter. I conducted a search of "computer" on Pixabay which presented numerous photos. I typically avoid realistic photographs on covers because they are hard to blend into the rest of the cover. Therefore, I clicked the "Images" menu option and chose "Illustrations". These are computer generated graphics which can be easier to implement.

On the first page, I found the image located at https://pixabay.com/vectors/text-editor-writing-document-text-1794110/, which can be seen in Figure 4.02. I clicked the download button and chose the largest PNG file size (1920x1945). Downloading high resolution files requires an account, but registration is completely free. I like the image, which displays a computer monitor with what appears to be a word processor on the screen. While this is very much a stock image, it represents the content of the book well. The blank page on the screen allows me some freedom for design. I also like the yellowish color behind the image. I can use that throughout the cover.

Figure 4.02: An image on Pixabay.

I opened this image within Photoshop, which opened in a separate tab from my template. On my keyboard, I pressed command-a (ctrl-a on Windows), then command-c (ctrl-c on Windows). This selected the entire image and copied it to my clipboard. I then switched to the tab with the template and pressed command-v (ctrl-v on Windows) to paste the image into the template. I was very fortunate that the image size was appropriate for my cover template. If it were too large, I could have clicked "Image" and "Image Size" within the Photoshop menu while I was on the tab with the image. This would have allowed me to modify the size as necessary to fit properly.

I moved the image to the right front cover portion of the template and centered it within the guidelines. Figure 4.03 displays this portion. I like the yellow color enough to stretch it throughout the entire cover. I conducted the following within Photoshop with the template selected.

- Click "Layer" in the menu, then "New", followed by "Layer".

- Title the layer "Background" and click "OK".

- Click the small square in the lower left of Photoshop in order to select a color.

- Hover over the yellow background of the image and click an area.

- Click "OK" in the "Color Picker".

- Click the "Paint Bucket Tool" in the left menu (if it is not visible, right-click the "Gradient Tool" and switch to the bucket).

- Click anywhere outside the image to make the entire background the selected color.

- In the right menu, drag the "Background" layer below the image layer.

- Double-click the image layer and rename to "Computer".

- Double-click the template layer and rename to "Template".

I now have a solid background with a centered image on the cover, as seen in Figure 4.04. I now want to add my title, subtitle, and author name to the cover. I conducted the following.

- Click the "Text Tool" in the left menu and draw a box around the top front cover area.

- Choose a white font color in the upper middle area.

- Select a font of "Impact" and size of 72 point.

- Enter the text of the title.

- Click the "Text Tool" in the left menu and draw a box below the title.

- Choose a white font color in the upper middle area.

- Select a font of "DIN Condensed Bold" and size of 50 point.

- Enter the text of the subtitle.

- Using the top "Move Tool", center the text as desired.

- Click the "Text Tool" in the left menu and draw a box within the computer image.

- Choose a black font color in the upper middle area.

- Select a font of "Courier" and size of 14 point and enter the text of the author.

- Properly label all of the new layers.

The typefaces and fonts I chose were very intentional. Typefaces are the overall design of the lettering, such as Garamond, while fonts are a particular size, weight and style of a typeface, such as 50 point bold italic. The title and subtitle I chose are sans-serif fonts while the author is a serif font. Let's digest the differences.

Serif: A serif is a decorative stroke that finishes off the end of a letter's stem. It is often referred to as the feet of the letters. Serif typefaces may appear fancier and more traditional. The font I chose for the interior was a serif typeface (Garamond 11.5 point). Serif typefaces have a history that dates back to the 18th century when stonemasons would carve letters into rock. Today, we see a lot of serif typefaces in traditional mediums such as newspapers, magazines, and books. That is why serif typefaces are typically seen as more classical and refined.

Sans-serif: A sans-serif typeface does not possess the strokes (or serifs). Sans-serif typefaces tend to have less stroke width variation than serif typefaces. They are often used to convey simplicity and modernity or minimalism. One characteristic of sans-serif typefaces is the use of simple, clean lines that are the same width throughout. This is the main reason many web designers prefer this style for on-screen use. The clean lines and sharp edges typically increase legibility for users.

The majority of people who will consider purchasing your book will only see a small thumbnail of the cover while browsing through Amazon or their Kindle store. If your title cannot be immediately and easily read through this image, it may be ignored. On Amazon, your book cover is reduced to approximately 500 x 300 pixels in the top left of your book sales page. It is even smaller within a view with other books. This is very low quality, so we need our titles to be large and legible. I wanted a bold and easy to read title which would "pop" during a cover preview. I chose Impact right away.

The Impact typeface was designed by Geoffrey Lee in 1965. It is known for having been included in the core fonts for Microsoft Windows since Windows 98. It is also available freely within Mac computers. More recently, it has been used extensively in various internet memes due to readability in small images. For my cover, use of all uppercase letters in this font make the title legible in any size of Amazon thumbnail.

DIN Condensed Bold is an Adobe typeface included in your free trial of Photoshop. It was designed by Manvel Shmavonyan and Tagir Safayev. It is clean and minimalistic. More importantly, it is compressed. This allows me to squeeze in an entire subtitle on one line without decreasing my font size below 50. While this wasn't an issue with my short subtitle, I still liked the condensed look. This will help with readability on Amazon.

Courier is a public-domain typeface designed by Howard Kettler in the 1950's. It was initially created for IBM's typewriters, and versions of it are now installed on most desktop computers. For my use, it reminds me of a typical typewriter output which was perfect for the author name within the computer screen on the cover. My last three books have included my author name within an image. I find this to be more unique than simply printing a name on the cover. In *Extreme Privacy*, I embedded my name on the camera lens focused on a map of the world, while *Open Source Intelligence Techniques* displayed my name within a typical search bar, as seen below. This is very much a matter of personal preference, and I encourage you to get creative.

If I have sparked an interest in font history, I highly recommend the book *Just My Type* by Simon Garfield. It opened my eyes to the importance of fonts within our lives.

Figure 4.03: An image over the Amazon cover template.

Figure 4.04: An expanded background created from the color of an image background.

Since I prefer a simple cover without too much activity, I think mine is done and is visible in Figure 4.05. Now, I need to create a spine. I conducted the following.

- Click the "Text Tool" in the left menu and draw a box around the back cover area.

- Choose a white font color in the upper middle area.

- Select a font of "Impact" and size of 40 point.

- Enter the text of the title.

- With the text highlighted, move the mouse near the border of the text box until the cursor changes to a curved double arrow.

- Click and drag until the text appears vertical and the numerical value is 90 degrees.

- Using the upper-left "Move Tool", center the spine text as desired.

- Click the "Text Tool" in the left menu and draw a box around the back cover area.

- Choose a white font color in the upper middle area.

- Select a font of "Helvetica" and size of 15 point and enter the text of the author.

- With the text highlighted, move the mouse near the border of the text box until the cursor changes to a curved double arrow.

- Click and drag until the text appears vertical and the numerical value is 90 degrees.

- Using the upper-left "Move Tool", center the spine text as desired.

The cover is starting to take shape, as seen in Figure 4.05, but I have a new problem. I do not know if the cover and spine content is properly centered within the boundaries of the template. I can click the "eyeball" next to the template layer to turn it on and off. This may allow me to see if things look appropriate, but I want the template visible in the background of all of my content in order to truly measure accurately. Consider Figure 4.01 which was previously explained. It shows me the boundaries of the template, but none of my content. I can drag that layer to the bottom of my menu to see my content, but now I cannot see the boundaries. We can correct this with the following steps.

- Move the "Template" layer to the top of the layer menu, as seen in Figure 4.06. This can be done by selecting, dragging, and dropping.

- Make sure all layers are visible with the "eyeballs" enabled. Clicking the eye or empty space to the left of the layer toggles this option.

- Select the "Magic Wand Tool" in the left menu. If it is not visible, right-click the "Object" or "Quick" selection tool and choose the "Magic Wand Tool".

- Click and select the "Template" layer in the right menu.

- Click the solid white background of the template on the back cover and press the delete key on the keyboard.

- Click the solid white background of the template on the spine and press the delete key on the keyboard.

- Click the solid white background of the template on the front cover and press the delete key on the keyboard.

- Using the upper-left "Move Tool", center each layer as desired. This is done by clicking, holding, and moving the content throughout the screen.

These actions allow me to see if the text and image are centered properly within the boundaries of the template. Figure 4.07 displays this view while Figure 4.08 displays the current cover without the template visible. I realize that the boundary lines are colored similar to the background, and that it may be difficult to identify them within a black and white print of this book. Next, I want to add my website and back-cover text. I conducted the following.

- Click the "Text Tool" in the left menu and draw a box around the top back-cover area.

- Choose a white font color in the upper middle area.

- Select a font of "Helvetica" and size of 12 point.

- Enter the desired text description of the book.

- Click the "Text Tool" in the left menu and draw a box around the bottom back-cover.

- Choose a white font color in the upper middle area.

- Select a font of "Impact" and size of 24 point.

- Enter the website text.

- Using the upper-left "Move Tool", center or align each layer as desired.

Figure 4.09 displays my final result. When you are finished editing your own cover, you should save it as a PSD file. Within Photoshop, navigate to "File", "Save as", change the "Format" to "Photoshop", and provide a name for the file. Save the document within your master book folder. Make sure you are providing a unique file name and not overwriting a current file.

While I suspect that my final cover will be slightly modified before print, I am satisfied with the overall theme. The images presented here are likely different than the final product, but I hope they give you guidance toward creating your own files. My final Photoshop PSD file is available to you on my website, along with all templates from this book, at the following address.

https://inteltechniques.com/selfpublish

You can download this file, unzip it, open the PSD file within Photoshop, and play with the layers. It could also be used as a starting point for your own book. Please play with the file to understand how the layers function.

I highly recommend labeling every new layer you create as you go. Figure 4.06 displays my current menu of layers. Any layer above another layer is visible on top. Keep your background at the bottom of the list so that all text and images are on top of the background. Be sure to hide your template before you create a final PDF in order to prevent it from being printed within the cover.

I offer one final piece of advice about cover alignment. Even if your spine, front, and back are perfectly centered within your Photoshop file and KDP template, that does not mean it will be printed properly. I have witnessed spine titling as off-centered text almost touching the edge. KDP print quality can be random. I have received almost perfect prints and awful cut jobs within the same bulk order. Because of this, I have altered the way in which I embed spine titles within my final document.

I have found that a small spine title which does not stretch from the boundaries presented above and below the text is more prone to improper centering. When my text almost touches the boundaries of the spine, I witness much better results. I don't have any specific reason this happens; it is just my experience. I suspect that a spine title which fills most of the width of the spine is easier to center than smaller text.

Figure 4.05: A completed cover with vertical spine.

Figure 4.06: A layer menu with custom labels.

Figure 4.07: The front, spine, and back content centered within a transparent template.

Figure 4.08: The front and spine content centered without a transparent template.

Figure 4.09: A completed draft of a cover.

Cover Background

I definitely cheated with my cover. I accepted the background color of my chosen image and applied it to the rest of my book. You may find an image you wish to use which possesses a background color you want to change. In my scenario, the text is almost washed out due to the light yellow color. I believe a darker color would make things "pop" more. Let's walk through the process of making my entire background dark green. I conducted the following within Photoshop.

- Click on the "Background" layer in the lower-right, which includes the image.

- Click the "Color Selector Tool" on the left menu.

- Choose your desired color, note the number (mine was #006400), and click "OK".

- Click the "Paint Bucket Tool" in the left menu. If necessary, right-click the "Gradient Tool" and select the paint bucket option.

- Click anywhere on the cover to apply the new color.

Figure 4.10 displays my new cover with the dark green background. While the printed and E-ink versions of this book cannot see the color, you can see the difference from the previous covers. At this point, I do not know which cover I will choose, but I am leaning toward this new darker option. I believe it accents the text and image much better than the lighter color.

Figure 4.10: A modified final cover file.

Cover Texture

My current cover is sharp, but a little boring. I like the green color due to the contrast with the white text, but it just feels plain. I typically like to use a textured background instead of solid color. When I think of green textures, I am reminded of the old chalkboards in school. Those boards also remind me of learning, which is the goal of this book. I think I want a chalkboard texture covering the entire background of this book cover, but I want it to be subtle. This provides an opportunity to explain the process of obtaining and applying textured images. Let's get started.

I am entitled to a free trial of Adobe Stock (stock.adobe.com) with my existing trial of Adobe Creative Cloud. Adobe Stock offers millions of royalty-free stock images, photos, graphics, vectors, video footage, and illustrations. However, you must either pay for access or launch a free trial. The trial includes ten free images, and these images can be used for a book cover (with some limitations). I searched "Green Chalkboard" and was immediately presented the file available at stock.adobe.com/images/chalkboard-blackboard-in-green/34836271. This seemed to fit my needs, so I downloaded the full size image, which was 5616 x 3744 pixels. This was large enough to bring into my cover design without resizing. I conducted the following to my PSD file within Photoshop.

- Select the Background layer in the right menu.

- Select the "Magic Wand Tool" in the left menu (fourth from top).

- Click within the dark green background within the image.

- Strike the delete key on the keyboard to remove the background.

- Click "File", "Open", and select the downloaded chalkboard file.

- Right-click the background layer in the right menu and select "Duplicate Layer".

- Choose the Cover.PSD file as the destination and click "OK".

- Switch to the Cover.PSD file within Photoshop.

- Drag the new Background layer to the bottom of the layer list.

My cover now appears as seen in Figure 4.11. The textured background eliminates much of the plain look. Choosing a matte finish for the cover may provide a nice accent to the chalkboard design with a rough feel. Figure 4.12 displays my new layer configuration. Notice that I renamed the original background layer to "Image" in order to prevent confusion.

If you were a paid monthly subscriber of Adobe Stock, you would have the legal authority to use this image for your book without much consideration. Fortunately, participating in a legitimate free trial with a limit of ten images, we have the same rights to the usage. Per their terms of service, the image must be downloaded and published during the trial for the license to be valid. In other words, you have 30 days to locate, download, configure, and publish any images desired for your cover. Next, let's make sure this image is allowed for use within a potentially profitable commercial book.

There are two areas of the Standard Licensing rules which apply to my usage. The first limits me to 500,000 copies of my book. It allows me to…

"Reproduce up to 500,000 copies of the asset in all media, including product packaging, printed marketing materials, digital documents, or software."

The next section limits my usage of the image if it is the sole value of the sale of a product. This does not apply to my usage, but it states I cannot…

"Create merchandise, templates, or other products for resale or distribution where the primary value of the product is associated with the asset itself. For example, you can't use the asset to create a poster, t-shirt, or coffee mug that someone would buy specifically because of the asset printed on it."

I feel confident that I am abiding by the rules. I created a free trial, downloaded one image within the 30 days, and used that image in my book cover, which was published within the 30-day free trial. I then canceled my trial, which bring us to an important consideration. You must cancel the trial before it ends (but after publication) in order to prevent a monthly or annual subscription fee being charged to your credit card. The following explains the process.

- Sign in to your Adobe account.

- Under "Plan information", click "Manage plan".

- Under "Plan & Payment", click "Cancel plan".

- In the confirmation window, select the reason for canceling and click "Continue".

- Choose "Continue with cancellation".

- Confirm cancellation through the email confirmation.

I consider this cover to be better. I know from experience that a matte finish might look best with this textured design. I believe this cover will be easy to read on Amazon, even as a small thumbnail. The spine will be easily read from a distance, even if shelved with other books. Having a texture will help mask light scratches and fingerprints.

Figure 4.11: A cover with textured background.

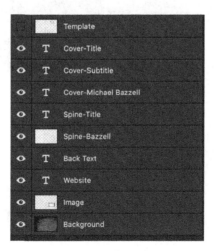

Figure 4.12: An updated layers list within Photoshop.

I like this cover, but I don't love it. The green feels off to me, and does not match the dominant blue emphasis within the image on the front. While you might be sick of reading about this cover, I am afraid I must make another change. I like the texture, but not the green. Let's keep the overall feel, but change the color to blue. I could cheat here and simply modify the current green texture into a blue hue. I could do this by clicking "Layer", "New Adjustment Layer", "Color Balance", and then "OK". This would present a series of color modification "sliders" and I could maximize the blue setting. This would make the textured background appear blue and may suffice. However, I think I can do better. I navigated to freepik.com and conducted a series of searches for blue backgrounds. I found one I liked at the following address.

freepik.com/free-photo/wall-wallpaper-concrete-colored-painted-textured-concept_3001819.htm

This image appears crisper with more of a blueprint theme than chalkboard. There is a slight texture, but it isn't as noticeable. More importantly, it matched my image well. I deleted the old background layer and repeated the steps from the previous background change. Figure 4.13 displays my final cover. Per the Freepik licensing agreement, I acknowledge that this image was designed by "rawpixel.com / Freepik", and I understand I am free to use it for commercial projects such as this book. My new cover is crisp and matches the blue tones within the computer screen image. The text is even more powerful than before. I am finally happy with my cover.

Figure 4.13: The final cover.

Press-Ready Cover PDF

Now that my cover is finished, I need to generate a press-ready PDF for submission during the next chapter. Fortunately, this is fairly simple within Photoshop, but we must pay close attention to the export settings. First, we should flatten our image and discard hidden layers. This simplifies our final product and ensures that undesired content is not visible. I conducted the following within Photoshop while my cover document was opened.

- Save the document as a Photoshop file.

- Hide any undesired layers, such as the template.

- In the menu, click on "Layers" and "Flatten Image".

- Click "OK" to confirm you want to discard hidden layers.

- In the menu, click on "File" and "Save as".

- Change the "Format" to "Photoshop PDF".

- Select "As a Copy" and "Embed Color Profile: sRGB".

- Do NOT select "Use Proof Setup".

- Click "Save".

- If prompted, confirm any warnings.

- In the "Save Adobe PDF" menu, change "Adobe PDF Preset" to "PDF/X-1a:2001".

- Click "Compression" and change "Options" to "Do Not Downsample".

- Click "Save PDF".

This creates a PDF file which meets the requirements of Amazon and other self-publishing printers. Your fonts are embedded and images are stored at full resolution. This may create a very large file size. I encourage you to name this file something similar to "Cover-Full-Resolution.pdf". It is very important that you do NOT save your current file over your master cover PSD. This version has all of the layers flattened into a single image and cannot be edited later. As long as you saved your cover as directed in the first step on this page, simply close the open file and discard any changes.

Next, repeat the process above while your original PSD cover file is opened. However, do not change the compression option (second from last step). Name this file something similar to "Cover-Resolution-Compressed". In the event that your cover exceeds the maximum file size for your chosen printer, you can use the compressed version in order to comply with their restrictions. This happened to me when one of my covers exceeded the 40MB size limit at the time. I did not notice any difference in the cover print quality. Submitting a full resolution cover is likely overkill, as printers compress the final PDF, but we should create and submit the best quality possible.

I understand that the nuances of Photoshop can be overwhelming. It can be a very complicated program, and we have barely scratched the surface of its possibilities. I have only presented the necessary basics here, but they should be enough to begin your cover design journey. If you do not want to download Photoshop and execute a free trial, most of the steps presented within this chapter could be completed using a free program called Gimp (gimp.org). This photo editing application aims to be a Photoshop replacement, but it is far from that. It works on Windows, Mac, and Linux computers. I was able to replicate my cover on Gimp with little deviation from the steps. The hardest part was identifying the location of various tools within the menus.

You will find numerous websites offering the ability to install Adobe products without paying for them. While some of these do present a successful, yet illegal, way to steal the software, an equal number of sites will install malicious software on your computer which will present many new problems. There is simply no legal way to install Adobe Creative Cloud without paying for it (after your free trial). In the interest of full disclosure, I purchase the annual plan to access all of the Adobe applications. My usage of Photoshop, Acrobat, Illustrator, and Dreamweaver justifies the expensive software licensing fees. Hopefully, you can complete the cover and export functions within your free trial.

You may also find a service offering free cover design within an interactive online tool. I have tested dozens of these websites which all promised free and quick cover art creation. While these options could help create an E-book version of your cover, none of them appropriately tackle the print cover requirements. Even those which promised to create full covers, including the back, spine, and front of your trim size, were all rejected by the KDP submission and analysis process.

There is no shame in hiring a professional cover creator. You will likely receive a cover which is more visually pleasing with no effort. For me, there is a feeling of accomplishment by completing the entire book by myself. Again, my final cover is amateur, but I am happy with it. You may need a professional cover for your masterpiece which will lead to mass sales in which I will never achieve. Hopefully, this chapter has convinced you to either tackle this yourself or seek professional assistance. Either way, the experience replicating these steps in Photoshop may be helpful in other promotional aspects in regard to your new book.

Cover Finish

When you submit your final cover for print publishing, you must select either a glossy or matte finish. This is personal preference, and I have experience with both. It is hard to explain within text how each looks and feels, but I will do my best.

Glossy covers tend to reveal deeper colors and provide more durability from light scratches. If the dominant color of your cover is pure black or a solid deep blue, a glossy cover will usually look best. The lamination process tends to bring out the darker colors and make them appear more "wet". White text on top of a dark background will pop from the page more, as the glossy lamination does not add any color or filter to a true white area. While light scratches will develop within the lamination, they are not as visually noticeable. Glossy laminate repels dust, dirt and fingerprints. Even when it comes into contact with greasy fluids, it is easily wiped clean. Glossy is the standard for most paperbacks.

I believe matte covers can convey a bit more professionalism or elegance in some scenarios, but colors often appear washed out or muted. I once ordered a matte version of a book which had a black background. The final product appeared slightly purple to me. The deep black color was filtered by the matte coating. It looked awful and I quickly switched to a glossy cover.

Glossy covers feel slick to the touch. They remind me of a photo developed from 35 mm film. Matte covers have a tactile feel which can also be beneficial. They remind me of older laptops which had glare-free screens. Some people describe the feel as "velvety". A matte cover finish is less reflective than gloss, providing more of a natural look to cover art. In my experience, a fingernail scratch or fingerprint on a matte finish is more noticeable than on a glossy finish. Matte is the standard for most young adult novels.

Overall, think of glossy as hard and defined, while matte is soft and artistic. Most of my readers say that the glossy versions feel more like a workbook which is designed to be abused and thrown around. The matte books feel more like a special product which is read and then shelved. Some say they are easier to grip due to their rubbery feel.

Today, most of my books possess glossy covers, including this title. While the background texture may have looked nice in matte, I suspect the deep blue would appear washed out. I also suspect the large white letters would not have as much contrast to the blue in matte finish. I wanted the best overall appearance and familiarity with my other titles.

Laminate differences can only be truly evaluated with example books in front of you. Ordering proof copies of your book in different laminates gives you the ability to compare and contrast finishes on your own. If you commit to a finish and change your mind, you can easily change to the other option. Obviously, this only impacts future prints, but know that you are not stuck.

Final Maintenance

If you know you are completely finished with the Adobe applications which you previously installed, you may want to remove them. The easiest way is to use the official Adobe Creative Cloud Cleaner Tool available at the following website.

https://helpx.adobe.com/creative-cloud/kb/cc-cleaner-tool-installation-problems.html

This tool is specific to Microsoft Windows and removes all Adobe applications. If using a Mac, dragging the various applications to your trash is usually sufficient. In either scenario, Adobe never removes all of the files copied to your computer. If you want continued access to the applications after the trial, the cost is currently $15 per month for Acrobat and $21 per month for Photoshop. I find this steep, but I am not aware of a better option. I write enough books that it makes sense to purchase annual plans for these two applications. Please note that we will be using Photoshop again when we tackle publication through IngramSpark. Again, I encourage you to finish reading this book before execution of the steps.

Some readers may believe they can remove the software, reinstall, and execute a new free trial. Unfortunately, this does not usually work. Adobe can see that you previously had a trial on your computer and are likely to block any future attempts. Advanced readers may consider installing Adobe within a virtual machine to generate a trial, delete the machine, create a new VM, and reinstall with a new trial. This typically does work, but exceeds the scope of this book. It may also violate the terms of service with Adobe.

It would be irresponsible to close this chapter without acknowledging the simplicity of this design and the likelihood that you will encounter unrelated frustration while creating your own cover. If you plan to sell 100,000 copies of your book, stop reading this chapter and hire a cover designer. I have presented this amateur attempt at a cover for two reasons. First, it would not be a very good do-it-yourself book if I simply told you to hire a professional. Second, I prefer fairly simple covers, especially if creating an E-book.

It will always be easier to hire someone to create your cover, but also costlier. The last professional I hired to create a fancy book cover cost me $1,500. I prefer my own approach, especially for a book about self-publishing. If you prefer to have someone create your cover on a budget, I recommend Fiverr (fiverr.com). At the time of this writing, there were over 10,000 providers offering cover design services starting at $25. Please remember two things: you get what you pay for and it can be quite satisfying to create your own book from cover to conclusion.

As a reminder, you can download my final cover PSD file used for the print version of this book from https://inteltechniques.com/selfpublish.

Covers Checklist

- Download a cover template for your trim size.

- Explore cover image ideas.

- Choose and apply cover fonts.

- Choose and apply cover colors.

- Choose and apply cover textures.

- Create your final cover for Amazon KDP.

- Export a press-ready cover PDF.

- Understand the features of glossy and matte finishes.

- Uninstall Adobe software, if desired.

- Download my final PSD file to understand the layers.

CHAPTER FIVE
PRINT PUBLISHING

Assume you have now completed the content of your book, exported a press-ready PDF of the interior, created your cover within the guidelines of the template, and exported a press-ready PDF without the cover template visible. You are finally ready to publish your book. However, this involves a series of decisions before you can provide content to any online printer. You must first decide which avenue you will take in regard to publishing. You can never reverse this decision, and it will have an impact on everything from online availability to royalty payments. In my opinion, you should take one of four options as summarized below and explained in detail later.

Amazon Exclusively (Without Expanded Distribution): This option generates the most royalty income. You are practically guaranteed 60% of the net income of your book, which is the highest I have seen with printed editions. However, your book will only be publicly available on Amazon. This is not necessarily a bad thing. Today, very few people refuse to buy from Amazon, so your entire audience will likely be able to buy your book. Another benefit is that your book will usually be discounted online, but you still receive the royalty based on the retail price.

Amazon Exclusively (With Expanded Distribution): This option generates less royalty income, but opens availability of your book to physical stores and libraries. You might see institutions purchase bulk copies of your book at a discount, which also translates into fewer royalties for you. The biggest risk of this option is middle-man book resellers may purchase bulk copies from Amazon, sell them for full price on Amazon, while you get the lower royalty (and they take a 20% cut of your otherwise guaranteed income). I rarely recommend this option.

IngramSpark Exclusively: The benefit to this method is that the print quality of your books might be slightly better than those printed by Amazon. This is not guaranteed, but my experience has always been that copies printed by IngramSpark printers have nicer covers and slightly thicker paper than those created at Amazon printers. I do not recommend this option for most writers, but there are a few scenarios where it makes sense.

Amazon (Without Expanded Distribution) and IngramSpark Cooperatively: This option presents the most global availability, decent royalties, choices of book printers, and the ability to own your own ISBN. This is the route I will take with this book and is the most appropriate option for most self-publishers. It gives us the best of all worlds relative to distribution. We take a minor hit in royalties, with a bit less control of how our books are purchased, but benefit from a wider audience. This method presents the most confusion and likelihood of making mistakes within the publishing process. If done right, you will reap the most rewards in regard to book sales, both online and in stores. Before we can understand the benefits of this strategy, we must work through the previous options. Let's dissect each of these in order.

Amazon Exclusively (Without Expanded Distribution)

This is the print publishing strategy I applied to my two most recent books (*Open Source Intelligence Techniques* and *Extreme Privacy*). Both of these titles are quite large (over 550 pages) and cater to a very niche audience. I anticipated the majority of sales to come straight from Amazon and was not concerned with the ability for readers to order copies from physical stores. This first option is the easiest to implement and can be the most financially rewarding. If you are looking for the fastest way to make your print book available to the world with minimal effort, this is it. Let's take a look at the basic details.

- Amazon account required

- Free ISBN provided

- Free immediate proofing tools

- 60% royalty on all sales (after printing costs)

- Available for purchase in 12 hours

- Print edition only on Amazon

- Not available in physical stores

- Not available in international catalogs

The lessons learned from this strategy apply toward the additional three self-publication options, so let's jump in.

Amazon Online Account: You are required to possess an Amazon account, but we should discuss a few caveats. The account should be in your real name. It should not be an account belonging to a relative or something you have used to order items in another name, such as your employer or a friend. If you have an Amazon account in your name which you have used to place orders in the past, it should work fine. Some authors choose to create a new account specifically for the self-publishing process. I prefer this method, as it provides some isolation from your shopping history and shipment location. Because of this, let's create a new account together. You can skip this first portion if you plan to use an existing account.

It likely makes no difference if you create a new account on the Amazon home page (amazon.com) or the Kindle Direct Publishing (KDP) portal (kdp.amazon.com). However, I prefer to create this new account at the KDP page.

- Click the "Sign Up" button on kdp.amazon.com.

- If prompted, click the "Create Your KDP Account" button on the login page.

- Provide your name, email address and password. Note that Amazon sends minimal spam to the email address provided, and this should not be a temporary, forwarding, or otherwise "burner" type of email. Provide an email address which you own.

- If required, confirm the code sent to your email address.

- Read and agree to any terms of service.

- Document your username and password.

KDP Account: You could use this new KDP account for Amazon orders, but I encourage you to preserve it solely for usage related to your book(s). While Kindle is in the name of this service, it also applies to printed books. This is the new home of both digital Kindle E-books and Amazon's print publishing service, formerly called CreateSpace. Bookmark kdp.amazon.com, as you will be visiting it often. Next you must update your account information by clicking the "Update Now" link on the KDP portal under the "Your account information is incomplete" section near the top. Consider the following steps in regard to each section of your profile.

Two Factor Authentication (2FA): If Amazon detects anything suspicious about your new account, such as an IP address associated with a Virtual Private Network (VPN), they may demand you to associate a telephone number with your account. While this is a bit invasive to privacy enthusiasts, this could help protect your account. When I created a new account, I provided a telephone number in order to receive a confirmation code. Completing this step sent me to the "My Account" portion of my profile.

Author/Publisher Information: Provide your country, name, address, and phone number. The address can be a PO Box if desired, and the phone can be the same you provided during the initial confirmation request.

Getting Paid: You will (hopefully) receive payments from Amazon when people purchase your book(s). Because of this, Amazon must have an avenue to send you royalties. Enter your bank's country, account holder name, type of account, account number, routing number, and name of bank. This may sound invasive and dangerous. However, there is little harm. Amazon likely possesses better online security than your bank, which is not saying much. This same information is also visible within every check you write. The numbers on the bottom of a check are separated within three groups. The first is the routing number, the second is your account number, and the third is the check number. A blank check will help you complete this form. Once you have completed this section click "Save" or "Complete Tax Information" in order to proceed.

Complete Tax Information: Since you plan to generate income, Amazon needs your tax details in order to legally pay you. Amazon will not withhold taxes in most scenarios, but they will absolutely report income to the Internal Revenue Service (IRS) for those in the United States. You must first select your classification. If you plan to provide your Social Security Number (SSN) for tax reporting, click the "Individual" button. If you own a corporation or partnership LLC (NOT a sole-member LLC), and plan to provide an Employer Identification Number (EIN), click the "Business" button.

Most writers publish individually under their SSN or a sole-member LLC. I publish under my corporation for taxation purposes, but I do not recommend creating an incorporated business for the sole purpose of self-publishing. If you are classified with the IRS as a Sole Proprietor or Single-Member LLC, choose the "Individual" option. Disclose whether you are a "U.S. Person" for U.S. tax purposes, and you should now see the Tax Identity section.

Tax Identity Information: Enter your full real name and any optional business or trade name. If filing as an individual, leave the business field blank. If you plan to provide a single-member LLC EIN for tax reporting purposes, provide the business name. Confirm your mailing address. Select either "SSN or ITIN" if you plan to provide an SSN or "EIN" if you plan to provide a business EIN.

Sign and Submit: Once you have completed all sections, check the box confirming you consent to providing an electronic signature for the information provided as per IRS Form W-9. Enter your full name and click "Save and Preview". Confirm all details are correct on the next page and you are ready to use your account.

KDP Bookshelf: You can now create your first book project. This can be done before your content and cover are completed, but I believe it is easiest when you know all of the details of the final draft. While logged in to the KDP website, click on the "Bookshelf" link at the top of the page, and then click "+ Paperback" in the "Create a New Title" section of the page. There are several sections which need to be completed, all of which are explained in the following pages.

Language: Choose your paperback's primary language, which is the language in which the book was written, not necessarily your native spoken language. I can say from experience that KDP will suspend any titles which do not conform to one of the listed languages. I self-published a Chinese translation of *Open Source Intelligence Techniques* when it was in the fourth edition through CreateSpace. Everything was fine until my CreateSpace account was migrated to KDP. At that time, KDP suspended the title and allowed no sales or modification to the project.

Book Title: This must be exact and cannot be changed after an ISBN is generated. This is why I prefer to enter these details after the book is finished. I am much less likely to make changes to the title after the work is complete.

Book Subtitle: This field is optional, but must be exact. It also cannot be changed after an ISBN is issued. All of my titles have had a subtitle, which is common for non-fiction.

Series: This is optional, and I typically never use it. This is NOT the appropriate place to announce a new edition of a title. This is used when you know there will be additional volumes throughout a specific series of books. I used this twice when I published the *Complete Privacy & Security Desk Reference* series consisting of two volumes (now out of print).

Edition Number: This is optional and only applies to additional editions of a title. As an example, my book *Extreme Privacy* displayed nothing in this field. However, *Extreme Privacy, Second Edition* displayed a "2" in this field. I never recommend placing a "1" in this field for a first edition, even if you know a second edition will be written later.

Author: If publishing under your real name, it should be placed here. This should be accurate and cannot be changed once submitted. You are allowed to publish under a pseudonym if desired, and the provided name does not need to match the name of the Amazon/KDP account. Only one name can be entered here, which can be frustrating when multiple authors are involved. The name provided will automatically generate an "Author Page" on Amazon, and any books will be linked to it. Choose wisely.

Contributors: This is the only area where you are allowed to identify others who were involved with the book. You can add additional authors or specify those who provided editing, illustrations, translations, and other services. I believe this section should only be used if the book was co-written and you need to acknowledge the other author. Unfortunately, this does not truly provide co-author status to the names provided. I co-wrote a book in 2016 and added the second equal author in this field. The final live product identified me as the author and the other person as a "Contributor". This required several support requests to have both of us listed as author on the Amazon page.

Description: This can be a difficult area to complete, and the precise wording is vital. This section will be visible on your Amazon book page directly next to your cover. The words will be read by most potential customers and should be both descriptive and enticing. If your description is not interesting, you may lose customers. This area is your most important marketing and promotion piece throughout the entire process. Your book could contain the greatest content of the decade. However, no one will see your work unless you convince them to dive in. I always struggle with this, as I do not have any marketing or promotion background. I am fortunate to only write non-fiction. I can drop a few hints about the tutorials I offer. At the time of this writing, my current description draft is as follows.

"There is no shortage of books about becoming a self-published author. Most titles try to motivate you to write your novel, focus on marketing strategies, and explore the occasional self-made millionaire success story. This is not that type of book.

This is a technical manual. It identifies the benefits and risks of choosing Expanded Distribution for a project and the limitations of Independently Published titles issued exclusively by Amazon. It clearly explains the nuances of free and paid ISBNs and the strategy of using both to ensure titles are available to every library and bookstore in the world, while maximizing royalties for copies sold on Amazon. It explains the differences between standard PDF files and PDF/X-1a:2001 formats and reasons why the latter is the best to use for final proof-ready documents. It includes all of the details the author wishes he would have known before starting his self-publishing journey throughout eighteen published books. The technical formalities of creating your own book are missing from the other titles in this space, and likely the reason many people never see their work make it to publication. This book removes the mysteries surrounding hardware configuration, software requirements, document formatting, book content, print publishing, E-book publishing, audiobook publishing, podcast publishing, book piracy, marketing, promotion, affiliate programs, income monitoring, tax reporting, and every other issue related to your own publication process.

This book lays out all of the author's experiences and how he chooses from the platforms available for distribution. The entire book was written while executing the steps which are discussed. While documenting the formatting of each chapter, the book itself is altered in real-time. All experiences are documented chronologically. As you read along, you experience frustrations and failures together with the author. All encountered issues are resolved before proceeding to the next task, and all templates are available for download. Simply stated, this book is about this book. It provides a unique experience which allows you to make it through the nuances of self-publishing."

This section can be changed at any time, but those changes can take weeks to reflect on your Amazon book page once the book is published. I prefer to limit this section to two paragraphs, and Amazon limits the submission to 4,000 characters. My submission above was 2,887 characters.

Publishing Rights: Choose the most appropriate option, which for most will be "I own the copyright and I hold necessary publishing rights". This requirement is to prevent you from submitting the work of others. The second option allows you to submit older books which are in the public domain. However, these will be scrutinized heavily and most are rejected.

Keywords: Provide any keywords or potential search terms which most relate to your book. These will be used by Amazon's search algorithm to help people find your book. Take advantage of all seven fields. For my book, I entered the following.

Self-published	Book
Publish	Author
Publishing	Writer
Published	

My goal was to anticipate the search terms of people interested in purchasing a book similar to this one. You can change these words at any time after publication, but it may take several weeks for Amazon's system to apply the changes. I encourage you to get it right the first time.

Categories: You should select two unique categories which reflect the overall content of your book. This area does not impact search results, but can influence your sales ranking within the specified categories. I located the following which could apply to this book.

- Nonfiction > Business & Economics > Business Writing

- Nonfiction > Business & Economics > Home-Based Businesses

- Nonfiction > Language Arts & Disciplines > Publishing

- Nonfiction > Language Arts & Disciplines > Authorship

Adult Content: Identify whether the book contains language, situations, or images inappropriate for children under 18 years of age, or should be seen by all ages. Answering "Yes" to this can severely limit your book audience and result in your title being hidden during search.

Save & Continue: You must click this button in order to proceed to the next page. However, know that saving your work adds this project to your Bookshelf. This is not a big deal, and you can remove a project without consequences, but this locks in a few things. Let's dive into the second page.

Print ISBN: This section requires some deliberate thought and explanation. I have mentioned ISBNs a few times, but have yet to explain what they are. International Standard Book Numbers (ISBNs) are numerical commercial book identifiers which are assigned to each separate edition and variation of a publication. For example, the E-book, paperback, and hardcover edition of the same book will each have a different ISBN. The ISBN is ten digits long if assigned before 2007 and thirteen digits long if assigned during or after 2007. If you want your book sold online or in stores, it must have an ISBN.

With this method of exclusively publishing through Amazon, it makes most sense to obtain a free ISBN from them. However, there are consequences to this action. First, your book will display as "Independently published" in the "Publisher" field on your Amazon page. I find this acceptable, but it immediately identifies your title as a self-published release. Next, you cannot publish this title anywhere else. If you later decide you want to offer the title on IngramSpark for better global distribution, you are stuck. They do not allow this ISBN within their system. If you decide to print your own bulk copies through a service such as Lulu, they will deny your request. They also do not allow Amazon ISBNs within their system.

My last two books possessed ISBNs issued by Amazon and I had no regrets. This kept my royalty rate high, as explained in a moment, but those books are only available on Amazon's site. I will never see those books within physical bookstore shelves, but the chances of that happening with my own ISBNs was extremely rare anyway. An Amazon ISBN is free, immediately available, and takes minimal effort. It may be appropriate for you, but is not the route I chose with this book, as explained in the final method within this section.

Publication Date: Most authors should leave this field blank if you are publishing your book for the first time. If you have a title which was previously published, you can enter a date in the past. However, you cannot enter a future date. There is no pre-order option within KDP for printed works. Your Amazon order page can only be created after you publish your book. The date the title is approved, after you submit this entire process, will forever be the publish date.

Print Options: This is where you specify the book size which was selected during previous chapters. This must match the template size of both your interior and cover. The default paper selection is "Black and white interior with white paper", which I believe is most suitable. You can switch to cream paper, but this it is slightly thicker and will require a cover template which specified that paper. The premium paper option is reserved for works with color images, and also requires a cover template designed for that option. You can apply the techniques explained in the previous chapter toward any of these options. Most books do not need a "bleed", which allows printing at or off the edge of a page. It is used to support images and illustrations. Most books use "no bleed" unless there is a specific reason to apply it. Changing the bleed settings will not change the manufacturing cost.

Cover Finish: You must select a glossy or matte finish for your cover. This is personal preference, and you should understand both. As mentioned in the last chapter, glossy covers tend to reveal deeper colors and provide more durability from light scratches. Matte covers offer a unique texture, but deep colors can appear washed out or muted. If you have the time, order a proof copy of each option, as explained later.

Manuscript: This is where you upload your PDF/X1-a interior file previously created.

Book Cover: This is where you upload your PDF/X1-a cover file previously created.

Book Preview: I highly recommend this free automated tool. After your interior and cover are successfully uploaded, click the "Launch Previewer" button. A visual representation of your entire cover is visible with boundary lines. This can help you make sure everything appears properly centered and that your spine will print as desired. From there, you can virtually flip through the pages of the book and make sure the overall appearance is as desired. I usually look at the footers throughout and make sure they are aligned properly. I also make sure my chapters all start on a right-facing page.

This view can be superior to the view within Microsoft Word, as the pages are aligned as they will be printed. If KDP detected any issues with your submission, they will be listed in the left column. Some errors are minor, such as image resolution and will not prevent your submission. Other errors, such as bleed issues, may prevent submission until you make modification. When complete, click "Approve" only if you do not need to make any changes. If you want to upload a new cover or interior, click the "Exit Print Previewer" button.

Territories: This is where you can specify which countries you want your book to be available for sale. Most authors simply check the "All" option. If you want to specify individual areas, select that option.

Pricing & Royalty: Finally, we get to the exciting part! You get to choose the retail price of your printed book, which determines the payment you receive upon sales. First, select your primary Amazon marketplace, which is "Amazon.com" for me. Enter the price you want for your book and allow the calculations to be made. I chose $14.03 as the retail price for printed copies. The printing fees from Amazon are $3.42 each, and the 60% royalty is determined by the remaining profits. If you purchased the paperback version of this book from Amazon, and did not return it, Amazon paid me $5.00 (thank you!). While planning, I chose $5.00 as my desired payment per copy for both digital and print. I simply played with the numbers until the amount was correct.

There are many opinions about the best way to price your book. No one knows the value of your work better than you, so I would not worry too much about the perfect price within the online pricing guidelines. I would focus on other related books within your genre and try to emulate the pricing. You want your book to be a good deal for the customer, but you also do not want to give it away. I typically decide on the amount of royalty I want to receive per book to justify the work and then choose pricing based on that figure within the KDP royalty calculator. This calculator can be accessed within your KDP portal or on the digital files download page at https://inteltechniques.com/selfpublish. You can always change the price later if desired. If you click the "other marketplaces" link, you can see your royalty and print rates for other countries. These figures are automatically generated by KDP after you enter your retail price, but you can change this if desired. I leave them alone, as they are based on current currency conversion rates.

With this strategy, all of your books will be sold through Amazon and you will consistently receive a 60% royalty. There are exceptions. Resellers may attempt sales at the full price or higher, which will not impact your royalties. Some resellers may sell used copies at a discount, which earn you no royalties and are based on physical stock of previously printed (and sold) copies. If you believe your audience will buy your books from Amazon, this strategy will earn you the most money in regard to royalties. If you select "Expanded Distribution" within the "Pricing & Royalty" section, that changes things, as explained next.

If you are ready to submit your book for publishing, click the "Publish Your Paperback Book" button. All of your content is submitted for approval. This typically takes 12-20 hours. If everything is approved, you will receive an email stating so. After that, your title should appear on

Amazon within 10 hours, and anyone can order your book. If you are not ready to pull the trigger, and I believe you are not, click the "Save as Draft" button. I never publish a book without seeing a physical copy in my hands. Before you publish, consider ordering a proof copy.

Proof Copies: Click on the Bookshelf link within your KDP portal. To the right of your new book, click the button with three small dots and select the "Request Printed Proofs" option. Select up to five copies, which is the limit, and your primary marketplace, such as Amazon.com. Click the "Submit Proof Request" button and wait for an email. You should receive a confirmation within a few minutes which contains a link to continue the purchase. You will be forwarded to Amazon, which will allow you to complete the purchase. You will be able to provide any shipping address and form of payment. Your books should arrive in 7-10 days. The cost for my proof of this book was $3.42 plus $3.59 shipping. Proof copies have a banner stretch across the back, spine, and cover which displays "Not for sale". Figure 5.01 displays the proof copy of this book.

If you are wondering how I have a photo of this book within this book, I reserved a blank page and added the image after I received the proof copy. I then created and uploaded a new PDF for approval. This was a bit carless, as I am assuming the new interior PDF is acceptable without ordering another proof copy, but I feel the risk is minimal.

If you are uncertain about the cover texture, I recommend choosing glossy and placing an order for a proof copy. Once the proof arrives, switch to matte finish within KDP and order another proof. This will take some time, but within 20 days you should possess a copy of each option. During this time, you can re-read the physical version of your content and look for any missed errors or required modifications.

Author Copies: Once your book is published, you can order discounted author copies. Click on the Bookshelf link within your KDP portal. To the right of your new book, click the button with three small dots and select the "Order Author Copies" option. Select up to 999 copies, which is the limit, and your primary marketplace, such as Amazon.com. Click the "Submit Order" button and you will be forwarded to Amazon which will allow you to complete the purchase. You will be able to provide any shipping address and form of payment. Your books should arrive in 7-10 days. The cost for my final copy of this book was $3.42 plus $3.59 shipping.

Discounted Pricing: The moment your book goes live on Amazon, it will be sold at the full retail rate. This may never change. If you see a spike in sales, you will likely see a drop in the price. Amazon typically provides a 7-17% discount on KDP books which are selling well. At the time of this writing, my book *Open Source Intelligence Techniques*, with a retail price of $46.25, is being sold for $39.39, at a discount of 15%. *Extreme Privacy* has a retail price of $45.99, and is currently being sold for $38.18, at a discount of 17%. I have no knowledge of how Amazon chooses these prices, and we have no power to force discounts. I only know that when a book is actively selling copies, discounts are usually applied. If sales decline, the prices rise back to the retail rate. I am sure there is some sales algorithm within their secret sauce which we will never know.

Figure 5.01 A proof copy from KDP.

Amazon Exclusively (With Expanded Distribution)

This strategy relies on all of the actions presented in the previous option. The only difference is enabling "Expanded Distribution" during the "Pricing & Royalty" section. There are many benefits and risks with this setting, and no author should select it without understanding the process. The following explanation is on the KDP website.

"Booksellers and libraries purchase paperbacks from large distributors. If you enroll your paperback in Expanded Distribution, we'll make your book available to distributors so booksellers and libraries can find your book and order it. We currently work with US distributors, but booksellers and libraries outside of the US may purchase books from these US distributors. It's free to enroll your paperback in Expanded Distribution, and it allows your book to be made broadly available outside of Amazon. Enrolling your paperback in Expanded Distribution doesn't guarantee it will be accepted by distributors or ordered by a particular bookseller or library. The decision to list your book lies with distributors and the decision to order your book lies solely with the individual booksellers and libraries. We can't provide details on which booksellers and libraries purchased your book."

This sounds fair. Amazon basically opens additional sales outlets for your book. In theory, physical bookstores can order at a discount, universities can stock bookstore shelves with your titles, and libraries can offer copies to lenders. In reality, stores order very few copies (if any), universities do not want our work, and libraries are happy to order direct from Amazon at a discount. I don't see much benefit to this program today, but there are many downsides.

Books sold through the Expanded Distribution option earn a royalty of 40% of the retail price, minus printing costs. This is less than books sold directly through Amazon using the KDP Print On Demand (POD) service. Many assume that the sales generated through Expanded Distribution would NOT have otherwise occurred directly through Amazon at the 60% royalty rate. I am not convinced.

Throughout the seven editions of my book *Open Source Intelligence Techniques,* I have tested Expanded Distribution and the lack of this service. Sales of this title are consistent without surprises when a new edition is released. The overall number of copies sold when Expanded Distribution was activated was almost identical to editions where the option was never enabled. However, royalties were very different.

Approximately five months after the initial release of the fifth edition of that title, I noticed that orders through Amazon were no longer being fulfilled by Amazon. There was a third-party book reseller who was fulfilling all orders, which seemed odd. After a month of this change, I noticed that my overall royalty rate had dropped from 60% to 40% for all sales. I determined this rate comparing the previous revenue to total units with the current revenue to units sold. The royalty per book sold had dropped 20%. This was due to a new middle man intercepting my sales. This reseller was purchasing my books at a discount since I was enrolled in Expanded Distribution and selling them through Amazon. Amazon still printed, stored, and shipped the books. Amazon received their cut. The reseller had very little involvement, but happily collected 20% of the royalties out of my share. I received no benefit, nor did my readers. This left a sour taste in my mouth. This is when I stopped enabling Expanded Distribution.

Another restriction with Expanded Distribution is the inability to quickly remove a title from Amazon for purchase. When I released *Extreme Privacy*, I chose Amazon exclusively without Expanded Distribution. A few days before I released the second edition of that book, I unpublished the first edition. Within minutes, the original was no longer available for sale on Amazon. The page was still present, but no one could buy it. This gave me comfort as I did not want people buying an edition which was about to be replaced. This is probably an awful sales strategy, but I prefer to keep readers happy long-term. You can have a fair amount of control of sales if you should ever decide to remove a book.

Today, I rarely advise enabling Expanded Distribution. If you truly want more global reach, consider the fourth and final strategy where we combine the services of Amazon with IngramSpark. In fact, Expanded Distribution already relies on IngramSpark for their services, so we might as well go directly to the source, and receive a higher royalty with more control. Even if your book is in all of the distribution catalogs, it will still display "Independently Published" if you possess an ISBN from Amazon. This alone will persuade many retail and physical outlets away from your book. We will fix this soon.

I have also witnessed a higher level of book piracy when Expanded Distribution was selected. I have seen evidence of this even when I did not release an E-book version of a title. Expanded Distribution brings in numerous third-party sellers which have authority to sell your book. In some rare scenarios, this introduces counterfeit copies which make their way through to Amazon. I have received emails from readers which included photos of the book which was purchased. Numerous indicators confirmed they were counterfeit, including missing barcodes, blurry covers, and improper page spacing. I have never experienced counterfeit books when I have published exclusively with KDP without Expanded Distribution or E-book versions. I explain much more about book piracy in Chapter Eight.

Is Expanded Distribution appropriate for any situation? I believe so. If you want to exclusively publish your book through Amazon; want stores to have the ability to order it for a customer; do not mind resellers taking some profits; and accept that you cannot control your overall royalties, it can work for you. It is the easiest option when you want to stay within the Amazon account boundaries yet still want some more exposure. However, I believe there is a better option. First, we must understand what the service IngramSpark can do for us.

IngramSpark Exclusively

I preface this section by stating that I never recommend this strategy. However, understanding the benefits of this service will help me explain the final strategy presented in a moment. IngramSpark is a publishing platform which provides Print On Demand (POD) and E-book publishing services. It is a popular choice among self-published authors because it provides affordable access to Ingram Book Group's (IBG) global distribution network. IBG is the largest book distributor and wholesaler in the United States. While Amazon's Expanded Distribution will eventually get your book in IBG network, it will still appear as an exclusive Amazon title. By allowing IngramSpark to facilitate inclusion of your book into a wider network, you usually see much quicker sales results. However, this comes at a cost.

The fee to create a book project with IngramSpark is currently $49. This includes print-only or print plus E-book plans. Once your book has been published, you can purchase your own author copies, similar to KDP. The following is a comparison of printing fees of IngramSpark versus KDP.

	IngramSpark	KDP
Page Count:	250	250
Print Fee:	$5.82	$3.85
Handling Fee:	$1.99	$0.00
Shipping Time:	25 Days Average	10 Days Average
Total cost:	**$7.81**	**$3.85**

As you can see, the costs to print your book for your own use with IngramSpark is double that of KDP. Now, let's take a look at the royalties of a book purchased through IngramSpark compared to the same title at KDP.

	IngramSpark	KDP
Page Count:	250	250
Retail Price:	$19.99	$19.99
Royalty Rate:	45%	60%
Print Cost:	$5.82	$3.85
Total Royalty:	**$5.17**	**$8.15**

If you sell a book through Amazon with KDP, you make $8.15, but if you sell that same book through IngramSpark, you only profit $5.17. That can add up quickly if your book sales take off.

That $5.17 rate also applies to any books sold through Amazon and fulfilled by IngramSpark if you go with this strategy.

As you can see, there are many reasons to avoid IngramSpark, but let's discuss some benefits. It will be much easier for a physical bookstore to obtain your book. You also have options to print hardcover and stitched versions of your book. These look much nicer than the standard perfect bound format which is default for both printing companies. However, these are also much costlier. I have found that very few readers are willing to pay a premium for hard covers or a nicer binding. I typically avoid these options.

Next, we should discuss quality. In my experience, books printed by IngramSpark will be slightly nicer than KDP. IngramSpark printers tend to create covers with deeper colors and interiors with consistently dark text. I have witnessed KDP versions possess inconsistent cover colors and text which had the appearance of a printer which was running out of ink. If superior quality is the priority for your own copies or customer orders, exclusively publishing through IngramSpark may be best for you. Neither will display a cover or interior superior to a book which was published through a traditional publishing house. Since all of these are POD, you are at the mercy of the chosen printer, ink status, and individuals controlling the process.

The process to publish through IngramSpark is very similar to KDP. You will be asked to submit the same types of data and can choose a free ISBN provided by them. However, this free ISBN will display the publisher as "Indy Pub". This ISBN can only be used within IngramSpark's environment and cannot be carried over to KDP or other printers.

I struggle to find a scenario where publishing exclusively through IngramSpark makes sense for someone. The only situation I can come up with is a writer who specifically wants to target physical bookstores and does not plan to sell many copies through Amazon, while staying within a single ecosystem without multiple accounts across services. I have yet to meet anyone that went this route. However, I see value in some of IngramSpark's services.

Instead of outlining all of the account creation and book details here, I will save it for the next section. We will work together through the process of taking advantage of KDP's generosity in regard to print prices and royalties while relying on IngramSpark's global physical distribution channels. We will also purchase our own ISBN and have options to order our own books from multiple printers.

Amazon (Without Expanded Distribution) and IngramSpark Cooperatively

Finally, we have arrived at the most appropriate publication strategy for most writers. In the first option (Amazon Exclusively Without Expanded Distribution), we had the ability to sell on Amazon and receive high royalties of 60%. If the vast majority of your audience buys from Amazon, it may be all you need. The second option added the ability to use Expanded Distribution, which made your books available to libraries and bookstores, but introduced the middle-man risk, which can decrease your royalties to 40%. The third option placed your book within IngramSpark, which made it available globally, including Amazon, but decreased your royalties unnecessarily. What if we could combine these tactics and receive the best of all worlds?

This strategy has a six-part approach, and each is explained in the following pages.

- Create an account with IngramSpark and purchase an ISBN.

- Upload all documents to IngramSpark, but do not publish.

- Upload all documents to KDP and use the purchased ISBN.

- Publish printed book through Amazon and allow to propagate in their system.

- Publish printed book through IngramSpark and allow to propagate in their system.

- Consider E-book options (next chapter).

This allows Amazon to make a page for your book within their site. Since you went through KDP, and did NOT choose Expanded Distribution, all sales through Amazon should provide a 60% royalty with fast and free shipping. Author and proof copies are available and you own your ISBN. IngramSpark will announce your title throughout the various order catalogs, which allows bookstores, universities, and libraries to order at the discounted rate. The Amazon page and catalogs will display your chosen publisher details and will not appear as a self-published book. You can order copies from IngramSpark to compare the quality and determine future orders. Since you already have an Amazon page, it will take priority over IngramSpark pages.

This process comes with a few additional fees, but the final product will be much more professional and have farther reach. If you only sell 100 books, you will make up the cost through higher overall payments from Amazon without sacrificing a portion of your royalties for the privilege of selling to a larger audience. Once you decide whether you will release an E-book or not, we can continue this strategy to get your digital book in front of a global audience. The Kindle royalties will not be lowered, even though we will refuse to give Amazon exclusive access to your title. This all requires very specific timing and order of events. We have a lot of work to do, so let's get started.

- Navigate to https://ingramspark.com and create a new account.

- Provide your name, email address, and a secure password.

- Activate your account with the confirmation link sent via email.

- If prompted, read and agree to the terms of service.

- Provide your business or legal name, mailing address, and telephone number, then click "Continue".

- Choose a security question and click "Save".

- Understand and accept the various agreements through third parties such as Amazon and Apple and click "Continue". I accepted all.

- Click "Finish Setting Up My Account".

- Choose your local currency and click "Add compensation information".

- Choose the appropriate option, such as PayPal or a bank transfer.

- If choosing a bank transfer, provide the routing and account number.

- If choosing a PayPal transfer, enter your PayPal email address.

- Click "Save" then "Continue".

- Add a credit card for future orders of services or books.

- Enter the card details and click "Submit" then "Continue".

- Provide either your SSN or business EIN for tax reporting and click "Save".

- Confirm Tax reporting details when prompted and click "Continue".

- Once you see that all details are accepted, click "Go to Dashboard".

You should now have an IngramSpark account which can publish books, accept payments, and report income to the IRS (if a U.S. citizen). Now, we can create a new book project. This typically involves a fee paid to IngramSpark, but online coupons often waive most or the entire fee. At the time of this writing, I searched "IngramSpark free coupon" and located a site announcing completely free setup with a coupon code of "SELFPUB". You could use this later to waive the setup fees from IngramSpark, but there is a catch which I explain in a moment.

- Click the option to publish through the "Print & E-book" package, currently $49.

- Choose the option to bypass file upload if presented. Mine appeared as "No, but I will enter my title information and submit files later".

- Select the option similar to "Print, distribute, and sell book" and click "Continue".

This should present the project setup screens, which require data similar to the details provided to KDP. I will walk through each, some of which present new considerations. Let's start with the easy stuff, such as the following.

- Book Title: The full title of your book

- Language: The language of your book

Next, we must choose an ISBN option. In the previous Amazon KDP option, we allowed Amazon to assign us a free ISBN. This works well as long as we only want to sell on Amazon. With this plan, IngramSpark requires us to either purchase an ISBN or accept a free ISBN from them. We cannot enter an ISBN provided from KDP. The free ISBN from IngramSpark can only be used internally and cannot be used with KDP. I never recommend the free ISBN from IngramSpark unless you plan to ONLY use their service and do not plan to submit through KDP. Since I want the best of both worlds, I will purchase my own print ISBN. This allows me to submit my book to any publication service and print my own titles through third parties if desired.

- Click the "Purchase to own from Bowker" link below the Print ISBN field.

- When prompted, create a Bowker ISBN account for yourself or your business.

- Click "Proceed To Payment" and submit payment details for the $85 ISBN fee.

You now possess an ISBN for your print title, which should be populated within the print ISBN field. However, this does not carry over to your E-book version. You must either buy an ISBN as we just did with the print version or accept a free E-book ISBN from IngramSpark. Note that a free ISBN from IngramSpark disqualifies you from using a free title setup coupon as previously explained. However, the setup ($49) is less expensive than an ISBN ($85). Therefore, I chose the

"Receive a free ISBN, owned by IngramSpark" option under the E-book ISBN field. This will not interfere with a KDP E-book submission, as explained in the next chapter. We simply want to reserve the E-book ISBN at this time without publishing anything. Now, we should finish the title setup.

- Choose "I own the copyright..." and confirm the agreement.

- Expand the "Show more fields..." option and enter your subtitle and author details.

- Expand the "Show more fields..." option and complete the desired fields.

The next steps are VERY important. Since I purchased my own print ISBN, I must provide my book details to Bowker and select an imprint. The imprint is the detail displayed after the publisher section of your book on Amazon and other websites. A free ISBN from Amazon would state "Independently Published" while a free ISBN from IngramSpark would display "Indy Pub". Your entry may default to your name or your business name, neither of which are typically preferred. I want to create my own new imprint, so I clicked the "Add Imprint" option. You can enter practically anything you want as a publisher imprint for your title, with the exception of other legitimate publishers. I cannot display "Penguin Press", as that name is already taken. I must be creative and search the internet for any potential imprint names. Once I find one which does not exist, I can use that. After numerous failed attempts, I finally decided to use "Blue Ridge Media & Publishing". Both "Blue Ridge Publishing" and "Blue Ridge Media" exist, but not combined.

This presents a new dilemma. If we planned on publishing exclusively with IngramSpark, they would transfer this imprint information to the ISBN provider (Bowker) and their catalogs. However, we want to publish through Amazon first in order to lock in higher royalties and free shipping. When we publish through Amazon, they will ask us for the desired imprint and verify the information with Bowker. If it doesn't match perfectly, Amazon will import whatever default imprint which Bowker has associated with the ISBN. This will likely be either your name or business name. At this point, Bowker does not know I desire "Blue Ridge Media & Publishing" as my imprint. To correct this before publication, we must update the account at Bowker with the following steps.

- Navigate to www.myidentifiers.com, click the sign in link, and log in to your Bowker account which was previously created during the purchase of your ISBN.

- Click the "My profile data" button, then the "My company" tab and scroll to the "Publisher Imprints" section. Enter your desired publisher name and click "Add imprint".

In my scenario, I added "Blue Ridge Media & Publishing" to Bowker and supplied the same details within the desired imprint with KDP, which is explained in just a moment. This SHOULD instruct Amazon to populate this information within your title when you publish through KDP. In my experience, it works 90% of the time. On one occasion, I had to contact KDP support and have them refresh their information from Bowker in order to display the correct details. While on the Bowker website, conduct the following to attach the details of your book to your new ISBN.

- Click "My Identifiers", then "Assign ISBN".

- Supply the title, subtitle, description, medium, format, genres, author, publisher, publication date, title status ("Active Record"), and price of your book. This should all match the previously provided details. Click "Save" when finished.

Back in the "Subjects" area at IngramSpark, I replicated my work from KDP with the following.

- Nonfiction > Business & Economics > Business Writing

- Nonfiction > Language Arts & Disciplines > Publishing

- Nonfiction > Language Arts & Disciplines > Authorship

Under "Select audience", I chose "Professional/Scholar (Adult)". I copied and pasted my description previously used within the "Title Description" field. Similar to KDP, I provided the following keywords.

Self-Publish; Publishing; Published; Book; Author; Writer

After I clicked "Continue", I was presented with one error. IngramSpark did not like my description. This is because there was a line break after the second sentence. Once I removed that break, my submission was accepted. Apparently, the first paragraph of any description must contain at least 200 characters.

On the next page, I selected the same trim size used with KDP and set the interior to black and white. I clicked the white paper option which presented the binding features. I chose "Paperback" with "Perfect Bound" binding. This is less expensive and more common with self-published titles. If desired, we can add a hardback option later, but that will require yet another ISBN. Similar to KDP, I chose the glossy cover option and entered my page count as provided by my final Word document or PDF. Note that this must be an even number, so round up if you have an odd number of pages.

I set my U.S. prices identical to KDP. This book was $14.03 per print copy. I selected the "55% trade" wholesale discount. To make your book available to retailers to sell in their stores or list on their websites, you must offer a discount off the retail price of your book. Any retailer ordering books will consider this discount purchase price and return ability. This discount represents the profit in selling your book for both the store and IngramSpark. The trade discount most publishers choose to offer booksellers is 55%. However, IngramSpark also provides the option of setting a discount within the range of 30-35% (minimum) to 55% (maximum). Applying a discount less than 55% will likely limit the sale of your title to booksellers. Remember that sales through IngramSpark are not very profitable. Instead, consider these sales as a way to reach a broader audience. Don't worry; this discount will not apply to sales through Amazon.

Next, decide your policy on returns. I chose "No" in the return category for a few reasons. First, bookstores are not likely to purchase numerous copies of your book in hopes of selling them. They are more likely to purchase a single copy at a customer's request. Therefore, a policy on returns would not be required in those scenarios. Next, I do not want books returned to me. If a person buys a book on Amazon and decides to return it, it goes back to Amazon. If a bookstore orders copies through IngramSpark, and returns any of them, they are sent directly to YOU. I don't want boxes of books to arrive at my mailing address. There is a third option allowing bookstores to simply destroy their copies and receive a refund, but I don't like that either. I prefer to state upfront to potential IngramSpark customers that I do not accept returns.

I entered these details within the United States option, which populated the other countries. This is where I see the depressing news. Each sale of my book through IngramSpark earns me only $1.12 compared to receiving $5.00 if ordered through Amazon. This is why I never recommend solely publishing through IngramSpark. Don't worry, only print sales from bookstores receive this discount. Soon, I explain how to make sure Amazon pulls from their own stock.

I selected the 55% option throughout the additional countries and replicated the prohibition on returns. I accepted the agreement about pricing. Under "Print Options", I enabled only the "Look inside" feature which provides a partial view of the contents to online customers. Finally, I set the publication date in the future. We can change this before actual publication. To be safe, I set it a few months from my current date.

I replicated these settings under the E-book option, including page count and release date. I set the pricing similar to KDP at $7.99 per E-book, as explained in the next chapter. The remaining pricing was auto-populated from this step. I clicked "Continue", then "Save & Exit". I feel like we should take a breath and make sure we are all on the same page.

As you can see, publishing through IngramSpark is much more detailed and granular than KDP. We still have a long way to go. Up to this point, we have created an IngramSpark account and attached financial information. We have added our title and obtained ISBNs for both print and digital versions. Next, we must upload documents, which is not as easy as it sounds. In the "Print Upload" screen, you must provide an interior and cover document for both the print and digital version of your book. Let's take each one step at a time.

Print Interior: The PDF previously created for KDP should also work well here. I have never had a scenario where my press-ready PDF was rejected. Use the "Print Interior" upload feature to submit the same PDF document which was uploaded to KDP. As a reminder, this should be a press-ready PDF/X1-a:2001 document, and not a generic PDF "printed" within a Mac or "saved" within Windows.

Print Cover: This is where things become complicated. I previously created a book cover based on the custom template provided by KDP. That final cover PDF might work here, but there is risk in re-using this file. Since IngramSpark uses their own printers and paper stock, the overall thickness of a book can vary slightly from the same title at KDP. This is especially true if your book contains over 300 pages. To be certain that I will pass inspection, I will create a new cover based on IngramSpark's template. This is not as difficult as it sounds as long as you still have your Photoshop file from earlier. I conducted the following steps.

- Navigate to myaccount.ingramspark.com/Portal/Tools/CoverTemplateGenerator.

- Enter your ISBN assigned by IngramSpark and the trim size, interior color, interior paper, binding type, laminate type, page count, and file type (PDF) of your book. This data should match the details previously supplied to IngramSpark.

- Enter your email address and click "Submit".

You should receive an email which includes a PDF cover template file which appears similar to the template provided by KDP. I conducted the following within Photoshop.

- Open the Cover.PSD file previously created.

- Open the PDF file downloaded from IngramSpark. When prompted, click "OK". Figure 5.02 displays this file within Photoshop.

- In the Cover.PSD file, deselect the "Template" by clicking the eye logo to the left of the layer until it disappears.

- Hold down the ctrl (Windows) or command (Mac) key on your keyboard.

- Click on each layer until all are selected, aside from the template.

- Right-click these selected layers and choose "Duplicate Layer".

- Chose the new PDF document as the "destination" and click "OK".

- Switch to the new PDF file within Photoshop, as displayed in Figure 5.03.

You should now see your full cover on top of the template. This is not very helpful. Similar to the previous instruction for our cover for KDP, I conducted the following within Photoshop.

- Select and drag the "Layer 1" layer in the lower right to the top of the list.

- Use the "Magic Wand Tool" to click and select the entire pink area within the back of the book cover.

- Strike the delete key on the keyboard.

- Repeat this process for the spine and front cover.

- Click the "Move Tool" at the top of the left menu.

- Select all layers aside from the template and drag them into place. You may find it easier to move one layer at a time by clicking the layer, then click and drag each layer into the appropriately aligned position.

Figure 5.04 displays a rough view of my scenario. The letters within the spine are too close to my boundaries and the various text blocks are no longer centered. These are common issues with IngramSpark which I need to correct. I conducted the following within Photoshop to the active PDF file.

- Double-click the "Spine-Title" layer to select and highlight all text.

- Decrease the font until it fits just within the boundaries.

- Select the "Move Tool" and re-center the spine title.

- Select the "Move Tool" and re-center the spine author.

- Select the "Move Tool" and re-center the back text.

Next, notice that my website is very close to the barcode on the back portion of my cover. This could cause IngramSpark to reject my cover. Therefore, I decreased the font and moved it slightly to the left. You are allowed to move the barcode to a different portion of the cover, but I have experienced rejections when doing this. Figure 5.05 displays my final cover for IngramSpark. I saved this file as Cover-IS.PSD, and then conducted the following within Photoshop to create my final print version cover file for IngramSpark.

- Deselect the "Layer 1" template layer.

- Click on "Layer" > "Flatten Image" > "OK" in the menu.

- Click on "File" > "Save As" in the menu.

- Choose a format of "Photoshop PDF" and click "Save".

- Choose "PDF/X-1a:2001" as a preset and click "Save PDF".

You should now have a press-ready PDF tilted Cover-IS.PDF. Figure 5.06 displays mine, including the required free space around the image. Bleed of the background is allowed, but no text. If you compare these to the documents which we created for KDP, you will notice a drastic change. You can now upload this PDF as the "Print Cover" within your IngramSpark portal. Note that a "401" error code may be present if enough time has passed since you were active within your account. If you see this, refresh the page and log in again.

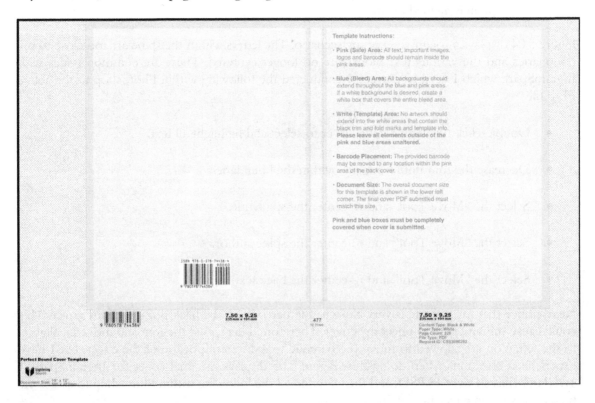

Figure 5.02: An IngramSpark cover template.

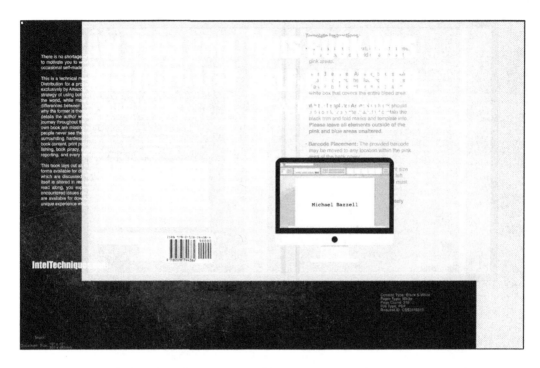

Figure 5.03: Previous layers imported into an IngramSpark cover template.

Figure 5.04: Centered content exceeding the boundaries of an IngramSpark template.

Figure 5.05: Centered content with appropriate boundaries within an IngramSpark template.

Figure 5.06: A final cover within an IngramSpark template.

E-book Interior: Unlike KDP, IngramSpark requires an Electronic Publication (EPUB) version of your book and offers no assistance with the creation of it. We will tackle this in the next chapter.

E-book Cover: IngramSpark requires a cover image for your book which only displays the front (not the entire Cover.PSD file). They also require a JPG format of this image, so I created one with the following steps within Photoshop.

- Open the Cover-Front.PSD file (explained later).

- Click "File" > Save As" within the menu.

- Choose "JPEG as the format and click "Save".

- Move the slider to select the highest quality and click "OK".

This created a file called Cover-Front.jpg, which I uploaded to the "E-book Cover Image" option within the "E-book Upload" section of my title in the IngramSpark portal. I do not have my interior file ready yet, so I clicked "Save & Exit" to save my changes. I now have the print version of my book ready for review within IngramSpark. I have not published it yet, and I do not want to do so until my book is available on Amazon. Therefore, let's stop the process at IngramSpark and refocus our attention to KDP. I realize that all of these tasks can seem overwhelming. At the end of this chapter, I will present a summarized checklist list which outlines every step required with this strategy.

Now that our book is almost ready to be published through IngramSpark, we should publish through KDP. The tutorial previously provided under "Amazon Exclusively (without Expanded Distribution)" should be executed with one exception. Instead of accepting a free ISBN from KDP, we want to provide the number which was previously purchased. Enter all of the details on the first page of your KDP book as previously explained. On the second page, conduct the following under the "Print ISBN" section.

- Select "Use My Own ISBN".

- Enter the ISBN assigned previously through IngramSpark.

- Enter the "Imprint" previously chosen and provided to IngramSpark and Bowker.

Continue through the KDP Print publication process as previously explained. When finished, consider ordering a proof copy to ensure everything appears as desired. This is an essential step if this is your first self-published book. Once you know that everything is ready, submit your book for review and publication through KDP. While you wait during the review process, we can pick back up where we left off with IngramSpark.

Back at your IngramSpark portal, continue the setup process with your print version of your book. Click "Continue" through the screens until you get to the "Upload" portion. Note that you may need to re-accept the terms of service by checking various boxes. If you chose the "Print and E-book" package, you cannot proceed past the upload screen unless you have supplied the print interior, print cover, E-book interior, and E-book cover. I will assume that you have created your EPUB file using the tutorial presented in the next chapter, and that you have uploaded all four required documents. This will allow you to proceed by clicking the "Continue" button.

The Validation screen conducts various checks similar to KDP. However, there is no interactive viewer which displays your final book. During my validation, I received the following common error.

"LOW RESOLUTION IMAGES IN FILE: We recommend color and black and white images be 300 ppi. For line art, we recommend 600 ppi bitmap images. For best results, please correct the issue(s) listed. You may refer to the File Creation Guide for further instructions on creating a compliant PDF."

This is letting me know that I have one or more screen captures which are low resolution. This is not an absolute roadblock; it is merely an informational hurdle. By checking the "I hereby authorize IngramSpark to proceed..." option, we can bypass this warning. I have often received this error. You can either navigate through your book to find the culprit(s) and replace them, or carry on. You will likely see this same error through KDP, which will also notify you of the exact image with the issue. Because of this, I rely on the KDP automated review process to better highlight any interior PDF issues.

If you continue through the process, you will be asked for payment confirmation and final submission approval. If you see an option for a discount code, SELFPUB should waive any setup fees. However, choosing a free ISBN for your E-book removes this option. Sneaky.

Let's pause before we submit anything and reconsider our timeline. Once you finalize the IngramSpark process, you are committing to the content of your book and the publication date. Be sure to change your publication date as desired. I typically choose the first available date closest to the actual date.

Any changes after publication will require an additional payment and frustration. Therefore, don't submit just yet and take another look at the ideal timeline for this strategy on the following page. The order of events is vital if you want full Amazon royalties. Failure to follow this guide may result in Amazon sales being fulfilled by IngramSpark. This is not all bad, as readers may receive better prints than what would be made by KDP, but your royalty goes down drastically as you are paid by IngramSpark. Your readers may also see shipping delays and unnecessary fees. Let's not take any chances and focus on the proper timeline. The following represents the steps I took for this book, using the techniques explained for KDP and IngramSpark throughout this chapter.

- Create interior word processing file (write the book).

- Export PDF/X1-a:2001 PDF file of interior.

- Create full cover files suitable for KDP and IngramSpark at your page count.

- Export PDF/X1-a:2001 PDF file of KDP and IngramSpark covers.

- Create Kindle and EPUB versions of book (explained in next chapter).

- Create IngramSpark account, provide all details, purchase an ISBN, and upload PDFs.

- Modify your Bowker account to include custom imprint and title details.

- Create KDP account, provide all details including new ISBN, and upload PDF documents.

- Order a proof copy of your book from KDP and ensure it is appropriate.

- Publish print version of book through KDP.

- After it appears on Amazon, publish the E-book version through KDP.

- After both print and E-book versions appear on Amazon, complete the submission process through IngramSpark for print and E-book versions. Provide a publication date of less than one week after the actual date for publication.

- Monitor Amazon, KDP, and IngramSpark for the availability of your book(s).

Once you submit your book to IngramSpark, it will go through a manual review process. If accepted, you will receive an email asking you to approve the proof. Clicking "Approve" in the IngramSpark portal presents a series of options. I selected "…approves this title for printing, distribution and sale from orders placed by my account and/or retailers…" and downloaded the proof PDF. This PDF includes your cover and interior, and is basically a replica of the content which you already submitted. I declined the $85 advertisement option and approved insertion of my book in IngramSpark's catalog. Within a few days, my print and digital versions were visible throughout various online retailers such as Apple Books and Barnes & Noble. Within a few weeks, my book was available for order at numerous physical book stores.

Hardcover Print Version

Until now, I have only discussed paperback print versions of your self-published book. If you choose a route which includes distribution through IngramSpark, you have the option to offer a hardcover version of your book. However, this requires a new project, setup fees, and unique ISBN. We can allow IngramSpark to issue a free ISBN, but that eliminates the ability to use a coupon to waive the $49 setup fee. Before you commit, decide if you need a hardcover option.

I created a hardcover version of a previous book. This was mostly for self-serving reasons, as I wanted my own copy of the work. I do not believe anyone ever ordered this option. The final product was not what I imagined. I had hoped for a beautiful hard cover with premium paper and a fancy dust jacket. While you can have companies create this for you, the default options at IngramSpark does not cater to this need. The product reminded me of a high school textbook cover with the same paper inside as the paperback options. Also, the cost per book was substantially higher. I will not be creating a hardcover version of this title, but I will explain the process in case it is right for you.

- Select the "Print book only" option within the IngramSpark portal.

- Choose "No, but I will enter my title information and submit files later".

- Choose the option to print your own copies or sell through IngramSpark.

- Enter the required details as previously done. Choose a free ISBN.

- Under "Binding", choose "Hardback", "Case laminate", and choose glossy or matte finish.

Everything else can be identical to your previous project. When testing the service with this book, my print costs were approximately $10 plus shipping per book. This is a fair price if you simply want to order a few personal copies, but the royalties with this pricing can be quite minimal. I do not see many customers purchase a hardcover version of a self-published book through channels which order from IngramSpark. I can no longer justify the time and expense of this option, but you may feel differently.

Your press-ready PDF which you created for the paperback version of your book within IngramSpark will not suffice for the hardcover option. You will need to create a new file. Let's walk through the process, which is very similar to the previous tutorial.

- Navigate to myaccount.ingramspark.com/Portal/Tools/CoverTemplateGenerator.

- Enter your ISBN assigned by IngramSpark and the trim size, interior color, interior paper, hardcover binding, case laminate, page count, and file type (PDF) of your book.

- Enter your email address and click "Submit".

You should receive an email which includes a PDF cover template file which appears similar to the paperback template provided by IngramSpark. I conducted the following within Photoshop.

- Open the Cover.PSD file previously created.

- Open the PDF file downloaded from IngramSpark. When prompted, click "OK".

- In the Cover.PSD file, deselect the "Template" by clicking the eye logo to the left of the layer until it disappears.

- Hold down the ctrl (Windows) or command (Mac) key on your keyboard.

- Click on each layer until all are selected, aside from the template.

- Right-click these selected layers and choose "Duplicate Layer".

- Chose the new PDF document as the "destination" and click "OK".

- Switch to the new PDF file within Photoshop.

- Select and drag the "Layer 1" layer in the lower right to the top of the list.

- Use the "Magic Wand Tool" to click and select the entire pink area within the back of the book cover.

- Strike the delete key on the keyboard.

- Repeat this process for the spine and front cover.

- Click the "Move Tool" at the top of the left menu.

- Select all layers aside from the template and drag them into place. You may find it easier to move one layer at a time by clicking the layer, then click and drag each layer into the appropriately aligned position.

- Double-click the Spine-Title layer to select and highlight all text.

- Decrease the font until it fits just within the boundaries.

- Select the "Move Tool" and re-center the spine title.

- Select the "Move Tool" and re-center the spine author.

- Select the "Move Tool" and re-center the back text.

- Deselect the "Layer 1" template layer.

- Click on "Layer" > "Flatten Image" > "OK" in the menu.

- Click on "File" > "Save As" in the menu.

- Choose a format of "Photoshop PDF" and click "Save".

- Title the file "Cover-IS-Hardcover.PDF".

- Choose "PDF/X-1a:2001" as a preset and click "Save PDF".

You should now have a press-ready hardcover PDF. Bleed of the background is allowed, but no text. If you compare this to the document which we created for the IngramSpark paperback version, you will notice minimal change. You can now upload this PDF as the "Print Cover" within the new hardcover project in your IngramSpark portal. Complete the steps there to finish the publication process.

If you replicate these steps in order to possess your own hardcover version of your book and do not expect to see any sales, understand the costs. IngramSpark requires $49 to create the project and fees around $15-$20 for the printed book and shipping. That means that your hardcover souvenir may cost up to $70. If this is acceptable, proceed. If this sounds unnecessary, I would skip it. My attempt at hardcover sales failed, but I do not regret the experience.

I am not able to create a dust jacketed hardcover for this title because IngramSpark does not support the trim size. If you know that you want this option, you must select one of the following trim sizes.

5" x 8" (203mm x 127 mm)
5.5" x 8.5" (216mm x 140mm)
6" x 9" (229mm x 152mm)
6.14" x 9.21" (234mm x 156mm)

The shipped cost of one copy of a 6" x 9" hardcover at 210 pages with dust jacket was $17 at the time of this writing (after the setup fees were paid).

Amazon Author Central

If you have a book on Amazon from any source, you should possess an author page. This is completed through the Author Central offering at authorcentral.amazon.com. If you published through KDP, your author name will appear within your product page. It may even link to other books you have written. However, you will have no control of the data present on the author page. Let's correct this with the following steps.

- Navigate to authorcentral.amazon.com and click "Join Now".

- If prompted, log in to your Amazon/KDP account.

- Click the "Books" link, then the "Add more books" button.

- Search for any books you have authored and click "This is my book" when appropriate.

After review, these titles will be added to an author page under your name. You can now modify this page and include links to your website, blog, social networks, and videos. You can also upload an image of yourself which Amazon customers will see both on your author and product pages. I encourage you to add a biography, which will also be present within these pages.

After your page is approved and populated, you will have access to some sales information about your titles. Clicking on "Sales Info" at the top presents the following two options.

NPD BookScan: NPD BookScan is the part of The NPD Company which measures print book sales internationally through points of sale. It is likely that not all your books' sales are reflected on this page, as NPD estimates they report only 85% of all retail print book sales. This bar chart shows copies sold of your bestselling books reported by BookScan for the time period selected.

Sales Rank: The Amazon Bestsellers Rank History page shows the bestseller rank summary of all your books. Selecting an individual book shows a chart of your book's Amazon Bestsellers Rank over time. Sales ranks are updated every hour, but do not include sales from any international sales. Sales rank is a relative measure. Your print books are ranked among all books on Amazon. Remember, this chart shows comparisons of your book with all other books in the catalog, so individual sales of your book might not result in a change in ranking.

I will use the sales rank tool in Chapter Nine to roughly determine the locations of my readers across the United States.

Content Modifications

Once your book is published and available to the world, you may want to make modifications. Fortunately, this is quite easy with Amazon, but IngramSpark can be a hassle. The following steps will replace your current print book within KDP without removing it from being available for sale.

- Log in to your KDP account and click the "Bookshelf" option.

- Identify your desired title and click the three dots at the far right.

- Select "Edit Paperback Content".

- Replace the interior, exterior, or both and complete the submission process.

You should receive confirmation of the updated content within 24 hours. After confirmation, all future printings of your book should possess the modifications. The exception is if Amazon pre-printed a successful book in order to stock multiple warehouses. After these are sold, new purchases will have the new content.

If you do not want your book to be available for purchase on Amazon, you can unpublish it from within KDP. The following steps will not remove your book page on Amazon, but should make it "unavailable" for purchase within 24 hours.

- Log in to your KDP account and click the "Bookshelf" option.

- Identify your desired title and click the three dots at the far right.

- Select "Unpublish Paperback".

- Confirm multiple warnings.

Note that this does not remove purchase options such as used copies. If your book is actively available on IngramSpark, new purchases may be forwarded to them. This is one reason why the option of publishing exclusively through Amazon without Expanded Distribution is desired by some. When I unpublished the first edition of *Extreme Privacy*, it was unavailable within hours from Amazon. Today, people can only buy extremely overpriced used options, as seen in Figure 5.07. The control of new prints can be beneficial if you often create new editions. If your published book is a new edition of another title, you can ask Amazon to place a forwarding "widget" on the page of the old book, linking readers to your new title. Figure 5.07 displays the forwarding option on the first edition of my book *Extreme Privacy*. I emailed the message in Figure 5.08 to KDP support to add this feature.

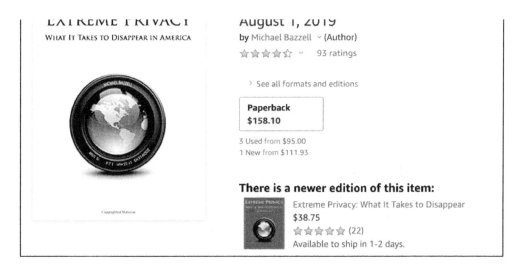

Figure 5.07: An Amazon forwarding widget.

I recently published the following 2nd edition of my book:

https://www.amazon.com/dp/B0898YGR58

I have unpublished the first edition:

https://www.amazon.com/gp/product/1093757620

Can you please add a widget announcing the newer product on the following page?

https://www.amazon.com/gp/product/1093757620

Figure 5.08: An email request to add a forwarding "widget".

Amazon also offers an option to combine your editions into a single page, which shares the reviews of all titles. However, I never recommend this. The idea is that a single Amazon page will be present for a title, such as *Extreme Privacy*. On this page, there will be tabs which allow a customer to choose an edition, such as first or second. In my experience, this confuses the customer and creates a scenario where an older book may be presented as a priority over a newer title. I also believe it is unfair to bring in reviews of an older version to a page which includes the newer edition. This can be misleading to potential readers. I encourage you to keep each edition of a book isolated from the other, with the exception of the forwarding widget.

IngramSpark allows modifications and unpublishing, but it is not as straight-forward. If you want to completely unpublish a title and prevent future sales and printing from them, you must contact support and state your demands. If you simply want to upload a new version of a book with slight modifications, simply repeat the original submission process. Expect IngramSpark to demand a $25 revision fee every time you want to make a change to your book. KDP does not charge this type of fee. Most of my books published exclusively through KDP receive several minor modifications within the first few months of availability. I have never seen any purchase unavailability during these submissions.

Finally, I should acknowledge pre-order options and restrictions. As stated previously, you cannot offer a KDP print book for pre-order. The date it is approved is the official publication date, and it immediately becomes available for purchase. IngramSpark offers a pre-order option, but that would ruin our plan to offer the book through KDP first in order to secure higher royalties. You would see the pre-order through IngramSpark on Amazon without the benefits of KDP. You can offer pre-orders of E-books through both KDP and IngramSpark, but I do not like the E-book to be available before print. I would rather control both and have them available around the same time. Therefore, I avoid all pre-orders while self-publishing. I do not believe the slight marketing advantage justifies the frustrations after deviating from our process. If pre-orders benefit your title, explore more about them at https://kdp.amazon.com/en_US/help/topic/G201499380.

This was a heavy chapter. Take some time to digest your options. While I may be repeating myself, I feel the need to summarize your two best options, which I present as "Amazon" and "Global".

Amazon: If you simply want to purchase your own copies of your paperback book and allow others to buy via Amazon, then the KDP-only option is suitable. You will still be an official published author, if that title is important to you. The entire process is completely free. You cannot publish your content outside of KDP, but you still own your words. Your royalties will be the highest possible, and payments and taxes will be fairly simple. Most of my books receive this treatment. The purchases through Amazon are always over 90% of all sales, regardless of which additional channels I add. First-time authors may find comfort in restricting the scope of their book to this simple option.

Global: If you want bookstores to be able to order your book on behalf of customers and a presence within international order catalogs, you need IngramSpark. This introduces the $85 fee for a custom ISBN and $49 setup fee without a coupon, but includes flexibility and opportunities which you will not find in the previous approach. If you want global reach and the comfort of knowing that anyone can get your book outside of Amazon, this is the method for you. The extra effort is minimal, but the outcome can be quite rewarding. While I chose this route, I expect most readers will come from Amazon.

The following page summarizes the checklist of events with the Amazon and IngramSpark combination distribution package.

Print Publishing Checklist

- Choose your publication strategy.

- Create a KDP account.

- Create an IngramSpark account, if desired.

- Obtain your ISBNs.

- Provide payment and tax reporting details.

- Complete the KDP title details.

- Complete the IngramSpark title details, if desired.

- Choose your pricing.

- Submit final interior and cover KDP PDFs.

- Order a proof copy from KDP.

- Review the final print version.

- Apply changes to PDFs if necessary and re-submit.

- Publish your print version through KDP.

- Publish your E-book through KDP.

- Create a new cover for IngramSpark, if desired.

- Publish your print version through IngramSpark, if desired.

- Publish your E-book through IngramSpark, if desired.

- Modify your content, if needed.

CHAPTER SIX
E-BOOK PUBLISHING

Now that your printed book is either available for purchase or ready to publish, you should consider an E-book version. Some authors ignore the printed option altogether and create electronic books exclusively. I believe this is a mistake, as over 80% of global book sales are still printed copies. With my own titles which offered a print and digital copy, print sales were approximately 90% of the purchases. However, my books are typically large reference manuals which are priced higher than most E-books. If you are writing a fictional novel or short tutorial, digital books may outsell your printed option.

As I write this, the world is still dealing with the COVID-19 pandemic. Thousands of physical bookstores have closed all over the world and companies such as Amazon often require weeks to ship out the latest bestsellers. On the contrary, digital book sales can be instantly purchased. Because of this, we are seeing a huge spike in E-book sales across all distributors. Some publishers are reporting up to a 15% rise in E-book sales. This does not come close to replacing paperbacks as the majority of sales, but these numbers may convince you to consider a digital version of your book.

I confess that I do not care much for E-books. I prefer physical pages which I can bookmark and feel. I am constantly disappointed in the formatting of digital books which seem to eliminate the value of the product. I see many authors submit the text of their content without any regard for the view of it within different electronic devices. I encourage you to do better.

E-books do have some advantages over print. Color e-readers, such as an iPad or Kindle Fire, can display images in color while our print options are limited to black and white. You can embed hyperlinks in order to generate internet traffic back to your website. There are no shipping fees and books are available to impulse buyers. Fonts can be changed; hundreds of books can be stored on a single device; and numerous features can assist those with disabilities. As I stated previously, we live in amazing times.

Ultimately, you should weigh the piracy risks of E-books with the potential benefits, which are explained within Chapter Eight. For now, I will assume that you want an E-book version of your work, so let's begin.

PDF Distribution

In 2012, I experimented with my first digital book distribution. I had recently published a printed version of an online investigation manual and possessed the final PDF which was uploaded during the publication process. I decided to sell it myself. I sent an email newsletter to my audience offering a digital PDF version of my book for sale. I created a PayPal purchase page and watched the orders slowly trickle in. I sent the PDF via email attachment to each person within 12 hours after purchase. This was a very manual process, but the orders were minimal. You could still replicate this process today, but it can become problematic if sales explode. It can get out of hand quickly if purchases outpace your ability to deliver the goods.

I typically do not recommend distribution of PDF versions of books. It is too easy for others to share the files with the world, and you have no reliable way of controlling the spread of your work over the internet. However, there are scenarios where it makes sense.

- If you prioritize publicity over sales, you may want your work to spread over the internet. Your book may be an attempt to generate credibility or authority of a subject. Maybe you are a tax advisor looking for new business. Publishing a free PDF outlining business tax considerations could bring in valuable new clients. If your book is an advertisement for services, online PDFs can be appropriate.

- If your work is a technical manual best read on a computer, then a PDF may be the most appropriate digital option. Traditional E-book formats such as EPUB or Mobi require third-party software in order to be opened within a typical operating system. PDFs can be easily viewed within most systems and allow easy copy and paste within the document.

If you want to give away your PDF content for free, you need a reliable web host. Ideally, this would be your own website or blog, which is explained later. Hosting with a free third-party provider, such as Dropbox, Google Drive, or OneDrive can be problematic. If the file is falsely flagged as a copyright violation or malicious document, it will be removed and your account will be suspended. Any download links which you had previously shared will no longer work. If you host the file yourself, you have more control. Additionally, it brings people to your own site which allows you to offer new content for viewing.

It is more likely that you desire to charge someone money to download your book in PDF format. If you anticipate sales higher than you can manually accommodate, you will need a distribution service. There are dozens of companies which charge a monthly fee to deliver your PDFs to paying customers without any interaction from you. Most charge excessive fees up to $100 per month, plus credit card surcharges. I have tried several of these services, and found the best experience through SendOwl (sendowl.com). It is the most affordable option with the most appropriate features for our use. In the interest of full disclosure, I did NOT add this book to any PDF distribution services. I only start here as it is the easiest of all options.

SendOwl is not a free service. The minimum fee is $9 per month to add your title, and the monthly $15 plan is more suitable for self-published authors. On top of that, you will pay a 2.9% credit card transaction fee on every purchase. However, there are some benefits over a traditional E-book. The following explains a typical scenario.

You upload the final PDF of your book to SendOwl. They host it on their servers. You connect a credit card processing service to your account in order to accept payment. I recommend Stripe over the other options. You possess a website which offers your PDF for sale. You advertise this address on your website or within other marketing avenues. When someone purchases the PDF from SendOwl, a few things happen.

With the basic package, the PDF is sent to the customer via a download link within an email message. The customer has a limited amount of time to download the document and the link then expires. The transaction is complete. With the $15 monthly package, the PDF is watermarked with the purchaser's name. This eliminates some risk of the buyer sharing the PDF to the world. You have access to all customers' contact information for future email blasts about new products.

There are problems with all of this. The watermarks can be removed. Anyone who plans to upload your content to book piracy websites will know how to remove any evidence of the purchase. Many readers may be offended if you abuse their contact details. If I purchase a PDF from you and you then send me weekly emails trying to sell me more stuff, I will not be happy.

Why do people choose this option? Two reasons: convenience and income. You already have a PDF, so your hard work is done. SendOwl handles all of the rest. You receive the entire purchase price, minus the credit card fees. If you have a technical manual at a cost of $20.00, your take is $19.42. That is a 97% royalty! As long as you sell enough copies to justify the monthly fee, this can be an option for some writers. All of the transactions happen behind the scenes, and you are not responsible for delivering the goods.

Overall, only you can choose whether PDF delivery is appropriate for your audience. I do not plan to offer any PDF versions of this book for sale. If I want to distribute PDFs to friends, family members, colleagues, or journalists, I can send a file as an attachment via email. When I do this, I typically add their name to the title page of the book within Word and generate a new PDF. This customization is a nice touch while also minimizing the risk of public release on the internet.

I close this section with another reminder that PDF distribution is typically not recommended for most books. While it is the easiest distribution option, PDFs do not transfer well to a Kindle or other E-book devices. Reference manuals opened on a laptop may work well, but a fictional novel in PDF is not desired by most. The majority of your readers will not want a PDF from you unless it is a large trim size with technical content. If you want to reach the largest audience possible, you must create a Kindle version of your book, which brings along many nuisances, as explained next.

Kindle Creation & Distribution

Amazon's Kindle E-book platform consistently accounts for over 75% of all U.S. E-book sales. If you plan to provide distribution through only one network, Kindle should be it. Amazon continues to make the E-book creation process easier, but there are still a few hurdles which we need to overcome. The Kindle Create software application should be used to generate a Kindle-ready document. Conduct the following steps to get started.

- Navigate to https://www.amazon.com/Kindle-Create/b?node=18292298011 and select the Windows or Mac version of the software. Download and install the application appropriate for your computer.

- Launch the application. If prompted, deny "Early access".

- Click "Create New" and "Choose".

- Choose the "Reflowable" option, then "Choose File".

- Navigate to the Word file of your book and select it.

- Click "Continue" and "Get Started" to begin working on your book.

- In the pop-up menu, deselect non-chapter headings and click "Accept Selected". Figure 6.01 (left) displays the options presented for this book. Kindle Create picked up several false chapters based on my chapter titles.

You are now ready to begin formatting your E-book, but you should first save a copy with the following steps. Save your document often as you make changes.

- In the Kindle Create menu, click "File" then "Save Project".

- Choose a location for your digital project and click "Save".

The Kindle Create software has an appearance similar to a word processor. Many authors have written entire books within this application, which I never recommend. I believe it should only be used as a modification and export tool for Kindle versions of a completed document. Let's explore the interface sections.

Frontmatter: Have you ever started a Kindle book which began immediately within the actual content? Did you notice that you could navigate backwards to see pages such as the title and table of contents? This is due to the Frontmatter section. Many properly formatted Kindle books place all of the formalities within a section which is first ignored by many devices. I believe every Frontmatter page should be properly created and identified in order to provide a smooth reading experience.

Body: The majority of the left column within Kindle Create consists of the Body section. These are all of the chapters and page breaks within the book. Your version may display only chapter titles. Mine, which is visible in Figure 6.01 (middle), includes numerous page breaks which identify the beginning of sections within a chapter. In a moment, I will explain why these are important.

Elements: The section to the right of your content allows you to properly format titles, subtitles, subheadings, and other types of content. Later on, I will use these to clean up my content to provide a better viewing experience on Kindle devices.

Formatting: This option allows you to forcefully modify elements such as font, color, and justification. I will use this sparingly as I continue finalizing my content.

For this book, I started within the Frontmatter section. I conducted the following.

- Click the "+", and then select "Title Page".

- Enter the title, subtitle, and author, then click "Create Page".

- Right-click the title page within the Body section and select "Delete Section".

- Click the "+", and then select "Copyright".

- Enter your name and year of publication.

- Copy and paste the text from your "Formalities" page into the box at the bottom.

- Right-click the copyright page within the Body section and select "Delete Section".

- Click the "+", and then select "Table of Contents".

- Confirm the auto-generated content appears correct and click "OK".

- Right-click the contents page within the Body section and select "Delete Section".

The Body section of my book is a mess. Since I inserted page breaks throughout the print version to ensure that new sections within chapters appeared on a new page, my Kindle version thinks these are all hard breaks which must also be displayed on their own page. Since Kindle versions are designed to flow without concern about page layout, I need to modify my content. I conducted the following.

- Right-click on any sections which are not chapter breaks and select "Merge with Previous Section". These typically possess a yellow dot next to the labels.

- Repeat the process throughout the Body section.

Figure 6.01 (right) displays my final formatting of sections. Readers can click within the contents page to be taken directly to a specific chapter. Most Kindle devices will begin the book at my author page, then the introduction, and finally the content. Now, I need to modify the content within the digital pages.

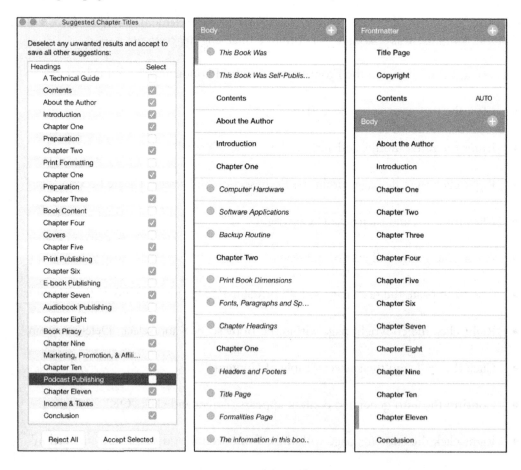

Figure 6.01: Various Kindle Create options.

Right away, I see a problem. My chapter titles do not contain the subtitles. The official title of a chapter is similar to "Chapter One". Instead, I want it to be "Chapter One-Preparation". This way, the reader can see the actual chapter titles within the table of contents. This is a fairly easy fix with the following steps.

- Click through each chapter within the Body section.

- Place the cursor after the chapter title in the document.

- Click the delete key and then the hyphen key.

This action will automatically update your Table of Contents page. Figure 6.02 displays a chapter title before modification while Figure 6.03 displays the final version after correction. Next, I need to look through every page and correct any spacing. Since I no longer have page breaks, I may find sections of text which need to be separated. I clicked on the Title Page option in the menu and then used my page down key on my keyboard to look through each page. I found numerous spacing issues such as one displayed in Figure 6.04. The page heading of "Dedication Page" should have a line break before it. Placing my cursor at the beginning of that line and striking the return or enter key is an easy fix.

| CHAPTER THREE |
| **Book Content** |
| Now that you have your template ready, chapters outlined, fonts placed, footers configured, and formalities complete, it |

Figure 6.02: A print version of a chapter heading.

|  CHAPTER THREE- BOOK CONTENT |
| Now that you have your template ready, chapters outlined, fonts placed, footers configured, and formalities complete, it |

Figure 6.03: A corrected E-book version of a chapter heading.

Next, I need to remove all text boxes which highlight text presented throughout the print version of the book. In Chapter Two, I explained how I enter the copyright details in my books. I then presented an example which had a text box surrounding it, as seen in Figure 6.05. However, Kindle does not know what to do with this box, so it displays it empty above the text, as seen in Figure 6.06. Therefore, my best option is to simply remove the boxes present within my Kindle version by clicking each box and striking the delete key on the keyboard. Note that I needed to place a line break before the text to display it properly after I had removed the box.

go back in time and change these words after someone is causing you troubles, so choose your wording carefully.
Dedication Page

I do not include dedication pages due to the privacy concerns

Figure 6.04: A spacing issue within an E-Book.

- **Declared Copyright:** It is not necessary to place a copyright notice in your book for it to be protected by copyright law. However, I believe we should all make are intentions of claiming copyright transparent. This book included the following line on the second page.

Copyright © 2020 by Michael Bazzell

Figure 6.05: A bounding box visible within a print version.

Copyright © 2020 by Michael Bazzell

Figure 6.06: An empty bounding box visible within an E-book version.

After you have looked through your entire book for line spacing, justification, and image issues, you should conduct a second review within the Kindle Create Preview option. This button, near the upper-right of the software allows you to choose a tablet, phone, or Kindle E-reader emulator. This presents your book as it will be seen from within different devices, which is helpful to test any page break modifications you have made. I prefer the Kindle E-reader view, as I believe it is the most common device used to read Kindle E-books. If you want to be thorough, test the pages within all three options.

The Theme option in the upper-right allows you to select from four overall looks of your E-book. I prefer the default option of Modern, but you may want to play with the Classic, Cosmos, and Amour themes. The Formatting tab presents font modifications, but these are extremely limited. You can select text and modify the bold, italic, underline, size, and color settings. However, I believe this should be done within the print version and allowed to be carried over to the E-book. I believe the two versions should mirror each other as much as possible. In most situations, I never use any of the features on the Formatting tab unless there is an error importing from print versions.

I also typically avoid any changes within the Elements tab. This section allows you to select text and modify the presentation. This can be beneficial if you want to emphasize a chapter title or subtitle, but we have already done this within our print document. You can also add features such as a large uppercase letter at the beginning of each chapter, which I find outdated. The Separator button can be helpful when you want to isolate two sections of text. To stay true to my printed version, I refrained from use of either of these options.

Once you approve the entire contents of your E-book, you need to export it. Click on the Publish button in the upper-right and save the generated KPF file wherever you save your digital project. This is the file you will upload to KDP. Unfortunately, Kindle Create does not offer an EPUB or Mobi file which would allow you to view the final product on your own Kindle device. This has always frustrated me. Fortunately, we can convert this file to open standards with a program called Calibre. Conduct the following steps to configure the software, which will also be used later to convert our E-book to multiple formats.

- Navigate to https://calibre-ebook.com/download and choose the version appropriate for your computer. Download, install, and launch the free software.

- Within Calibre, enter the "Preferences" option within the menu, click the "Plugins" button near the bottom, then "Get new plugins".

- In the "Filter by name" field, enter "KFX".

- Click each option and then the "Install" button. After both KFX plugin features are installed, restart Calibre.

- Click "Add Books" and select your KFX file previously created.

- Right-click the book within Calibre, highlight "Convert Books", select the "Convert Individually" option, set the output format as "MOBI", and click "OK".

- Connect your Kindle device to your computer. Once the device is recognized, right-click your title, highlight "Send to device", then select "Send to main memory".

You should now be able to view your book within your Kindle device. It is likely that there will be some minor formatting errors due to the limited capabilities of Calibre, but you can still test the content. I typically take a quick glance to make sure the text is accurate and chapters all begin on a new page. Note that this version will not be as properly structured as the KFX file which will be submitted to KDP. This technique simply allows us to make sure our content is correct.

You should now consider your publication strategy. If you have already published your print book with your own ISBN, you can publish the Kindle version with its own free ISBN issued by KDP. I do NOT recommend publishing the Kindle version before the print option. Amazon may refuse your print version with an outside ISBN since a similar title already exists. Amazon always gives preference to their own ISBNs and titles, so we should always publish Kindle versions after the print edition is publicly available on Amazon. My timeline so far with this book is as follows.

- Purchase the ISBN from IngramSpark.

- Publish the print book through KDP with the IngramSpark ISBN.

- Publish the Kindle version through KDP with ISBN issued from KDP.

- Publish the print book through IngramSpark.

If you are ready to publish your first E-book, let's walk through the process together.

- Navigate to your KDP account and select the "Bookshelf" link.

- Within your book's entry, click the "Create Kindle E-book" option.

- Confirm the details, which should mirror the print version.

- If desired, choose the "I am ready to release my book now" option.

- Click "Save and Continue".

On the second page, you must first make a decision about Digital Rights Management (DRM). DRM is software restrictions which are intended to inhibit unauthorized distribution of the Kindle file of your book. Some authors want to encourage readers to share their work for free and choose not to have DRM applied to their book. Others enable this feature to discourage piracy. If you choose DRM, customers will still be able to lend the book to another user for a short period of time or purchase the book as a gift for another user from the Kindle store.

Once you publish your book, you cannot change the DRM setting, so let's digest our options. First, DRM does not prevent unauthorized copying and distribution of your book. Piracy advocates can easily remove the protection and freely share your content within minutes. Typically, DRM keeps honest people honest and does very little to stop piracy. I applied DRM to all of my Kindle releases, and all of those titles were found without DRM protection within 30 days of release. If you are writing a book with the hopes of people sharing your content, disable DRM. If you want to protect your content as much as possible to encourage more sales than free copies, consider enabling DRM.

After you have chosen your desired DRM setting, upload the KPF file generated by Kindle Create and the JPG file of your cover. If you do not have a JPG of the cover, open Photoshop, crop your cover, choose "Export", then "Export As", and create a JPG file at least 1000 pixels in length. Click "Launch Previewer" in order to review your final submission. If you see any issues, correct them though Kindle Create and export a new file. Afterward, import this into the KDP Kindle submission process.

Unless you have purchased an ISBN specifically for the E-book version of your title, leave the bottom field blank. Kindle versions do not require an ISBN, and Amazon maintains the control numbers of these titles. Finally, it is time to consider pricing and exclusivity. Take these options seriously, as they all have catches.

KDP Select: You will be offered enrollment of your title in the KDP select program. Doing so presents higher royalty rates within a few countries and inclusion within Kindle Unlimited (KU) and the Kindle Owners' Lending Library (KOLL). With these, you can earn a share of the KDP Select Global Fund based on how many pages KU or KOLL customers read of your book. Enrollment in KDP Select requires exclusivity with Amazon. You cannot publish an E-book within any other platform.

Kindle Unlimited (KU): KU is a subscription service which allows users to read as many books as desired and keep them as long as they want for a monthly subscription fee. If you have a book enrolled in KDP Select, it will automatically be enrolled in KU. It will also be enrolled in the Kindle Owners' Lending Library (KOLL). When customers subscribe to KU, they will see a badge next to your book indicating the book is available in KU. They can also visit Amazon's Kindle Unlimited page and see available books there. You will receive an appropriate share of the KDP Select Global Fund as individual customers read pages in your book for the first time.

Kindle Owners' Lending Library (KOLL): Kindle owners with Amazon Prime memberships can choose from thousands of books to read for free once a month from KOLL. KOLL is different from the Lending for Kindle feature, which allows readers to lend digital books to their friends and family after buying them on the Amazon.com Kindle Store. Books eligible for KOLL will have an Amazon Prime badge for customers to see when they search and browse for books on their Kindle devices or on Amazon.com. Customers can read a KOLL book as many times as they like, but they can only read one title per month, one at a time. However, KOLL customers can keep reading a book for as long as they want. Every time a unique customer reads pages in your book for the first time, you will be eligible for small royalties.

There is a lot to digest here, so I hope to provide some real-world insight. KDP Select is a way for Amazon to prevent you from publishing your E-book within any other market. In return, they offer a few perks. People can read your book for free if they are enrolled within these paid programs. Amazon then shares a portion of the fees paid by these readers to the authors which have books read by the customers. In my experience, this is a minimal amount of royalties. In most cases, it is pennies per month unless your book becomes very popular. I believe you have three options, as outlined below.

Kindle Version (Exclusively) With KDP Select: This is very common for new authors who want maximum Amazon exposure. They understand that the majority of E-book customers have a Kindle and do not care about availability on Apple and other networks. They like the idea of their books being shared with others for free and very small royalties from those who read within various Amazon subscription programs. Priority is placed on exposure instead of income.

Kindle Version (Exclusively) Without KDP Select: This is an easy way to get your E-book on Amazon without catering to the demands of non-Kindle publication services (discussed soon). Anyone who wants to obtain your book from Amazon must pay the price of the E-book. There are no free options or abilities to give away books. This is appropriate for those who want more control of their titles without concern about exposure. You are free to later distribute through other publishers as you please.

Kindle Version (Non-Exclusively) Without KDP Select: This is my desired option. I have published this E-book through KDP and it is available on Amazon for use with a Kindle device. By not enrolling in KDP Select, I can publish this book through other channels, which I have. It is not available for free on Amazon, and potential readers must pay my selected price to obtain the book. Amazon does not have exclusive rights of my words.

Territories: Similar to the print version, you can select the areas of the world in which readers can purchase your E-book. I selected "All".

Royalty and Pricing: This section immediately presents a surprising option. You must select whether you want a 70% royalty or a 35% royalty. This seems like a no-brainer, but as always, there are catches. If you choose the 70% option, your book must be priced between $2.99 and $9.99 USD. For most people, this is acceptable. Few people pay more than $9.99 for an E-book, unless it is a niche topic. As an example, my *Extreme Privacy* book is 565 pages with a print retail of $45. If I sold it for $9.99 in E-book format, it would eliminate much of the incentive to buy the printed guide. If I sell the E-book for anything more than $10, I only get 35% of the royalties. Wait, there is more.

If you choose the 70% royalty rate, you are required to enroll your book in Amazon's Kindle Book Lending program. Anyone who purchases your title can lend it to others for 14 days each. I don't find this to be a negative option, as it raises awareness of your work without much risk of lost sales.

Most Kindle authors price their E-book between $2.99 and $9.99 and select the 70% royalty. I fit into this scenario with this book. Don't stress too much over all of the options. Keep it simple and focus your attention on promoting your book. Don't dwell too much over the royalties of digital products.

Free book promotion: After your E-book is live on Amazon, you may wish to offer a free book promotion. This allows Kindle customers to download and read your book without any payment (or any royalty). Some authors do this to generate buzz around a new title while others use it as a way for their friends and family to get the book for free. If you believe you would benefit from such a promotion, there are two ways to do it.

If your title is enrolled in KDP Select, Amazon allows you to execute a free book promotion on that title. Amazon limits the number of days that your book can be listed as free. You can choose to offer any book enrolled in KDP Select free to readers for up to 5 days out of each 90-day KDP Select enrollment period. You can use all 5 days at once, or you can spread the five days out over 90 days by using one day at a time until all five are used up. To set up a free book promotion, conduct the following.

- In your KDP Bookshelf, click on the three dots to the right of your book.

- Choose "KDP Select Info".

- Under "Run a Price Promotion", select "Free Book Promotion".

- Click "Create a New Free Book Promotion".

- Enter the desired start and end date and click "Save".

If your book is not enrolled in KDP Select, but you would like to promote it for free, then you must rely on Amazon to price match your book. This is a workaround which only functions if you have your book available on another platform. The following steps are never guaranteed to work, but usually succeed in a free Kindle promotion.

- Click the three dots to the right of your book in your KDP account.

- Select "Edit E-book pricing".

- Set the list price to $0.99 and click "Publish Your Kindle E-book".

- Log in to your account on Apple, Nook, or Kobo (explained in a moment) and set the price of the same title to $0.00.

- Contact KDP support through your account portal and request a "price match". Include a link to your book available for free on the other platform, as well as a link to your book's Amazon page.

Amazon is not obligated to change the price of your book. They may do so slowly, or not at all. It is best to initiate this process well before you desire it as an option. What did I do? I chose the "Kindle Version (Non-Exclusively) Without KDP Select" option previously presented with a 70% royalty rate and a cost of $7.41 per E-book. I am not enrolled in KU or KOLL. I did not pursue a price match to offer a free download. If you purchased the Kindle version, I received a $5.00 royalty payment after delivery fees (thank you!). This allows me to pursue other sales avenues by not authorizing Amazon exclusive rights to digital distribution.

Once you have selected the royalty options appropriate for your title, click the "Publish your Kindle book" button. Within 24 hours, you will likely see it available for purchase within Amazon. If you already have the print version active, the Kindle edition should be on the same purchase page, which is desired.

Finally, it is important to note that you can upload your Word document directly within KDP for conversion into a Kindle file. However, I have found this process to be problematic more often than it is smooth. I believe the Kindle Create experience offers more control of your work. Now that you have print and digital editions available on Amazon, let's explore additional sales opportunities.

IngramSpark E-book Creation & Distribution

If you chose the KDP and IngramSpark combination print distribution option previously presented, you likely already know that IngramSpark offers a print and E-book package at the same rate as the print-only option. If you have released a Kindle version, I see no reason to ignore the IngramSpark option to get your E-book to other outlets such as Apple and Barnes & Noble. Unlike KDP, IngramSpark offers almost no assistance with the E-book creation process. You are responsible for converting your Word document into an EPUB file. Fortunately, we can easily create this ourselves. I present two options in order of convenience to most granular detail. First, I recommend removing some content from your print interior through Word. I conducted the following.

- Remove the Table of Contents section.

- Remove the Index section.

These actions prevent the EPUB process from attempting to include data which is unnecessary. The Table of Contents applies to page numbers in the printed version and is not applicable within a flowable E-book. The final file can be searched by keyword within E-book readers, which makes the Index redundant and unnecessary.

Draft2Digital: Many authors prefer the Draft2Digital online EPUB conversion process. It requires no software and is fairly automated. It also includes a preview of your final product before download of any files. The intent of this service is to facilitate sales of your E-book, but they transparently offer a free conversion tool which does not require final submission. I conducted the following steps to create an EPUB file acceptable by IngramSpark.

- Navigate to draft2digital.com and click the "Sign up" button.

- Complete the required form, submit the data, and log in to your account.

- Click the option to "Add new book".

- Upload your cover art and complete the details such as title, name, etc.

- Click "Start E-book".

- Upload your book's interior Word document and add your description.

- Choose the option for a free ISBN and click "Save and Continue".

The next screen will analyze your file and attempt to identify the chapter breaks. If everything looks OK, proceed. Mine appeared as visible in Figure 6.07. If your chapters appear incorrect, you can slightly modify things by pressing the "Help! These aren't my chapters" button. This presents additional layout options which may be more appropriate. If none of these solves your situation, you will need to modify the Word file more. Since I have already included an author page and introduction, I did not add any "End matter".

Continuing through the process presents an interactive E-book reader containing your submitted content. Browse through the pages and make sure the contents appear appropriate. With the links to the right, download an EPUB, Mobi, and PDF version of your converted work. The EPUB version can be uploaded to IngramSpark as explained in the previous chapter.

If you no longer want your book present within the Draft2Digital site, you can completely delete it. I did this with the following steps.

- Click the "My Books" button on the home page.

- Select the book.

- Click the grey "Delete Book" button and confirm removal.

All evidence of your work is now gone. You can maintain this online account for future conversions if desired.

Calibre: If Draft2Digital no longer offers a free conversion service by the time you read this, or you prefer to conduct your own file creation, then Calibre is a great option. I conducted the following in order to create my own EPUB file locally.

- Navigate to https://calibre-ebook.com/download.

- Download and install the software appropriate for your operating system.

- Within Calibre, click the "Add Books" button and select your modified Word file.

- Right-click this new file and select "Convert books" then "Convert individually".

- Change the output format to "EPUB".

- Select your cover image, as seen in Figure 6.08.

- Enter your name and publisher details, and then click "OK".

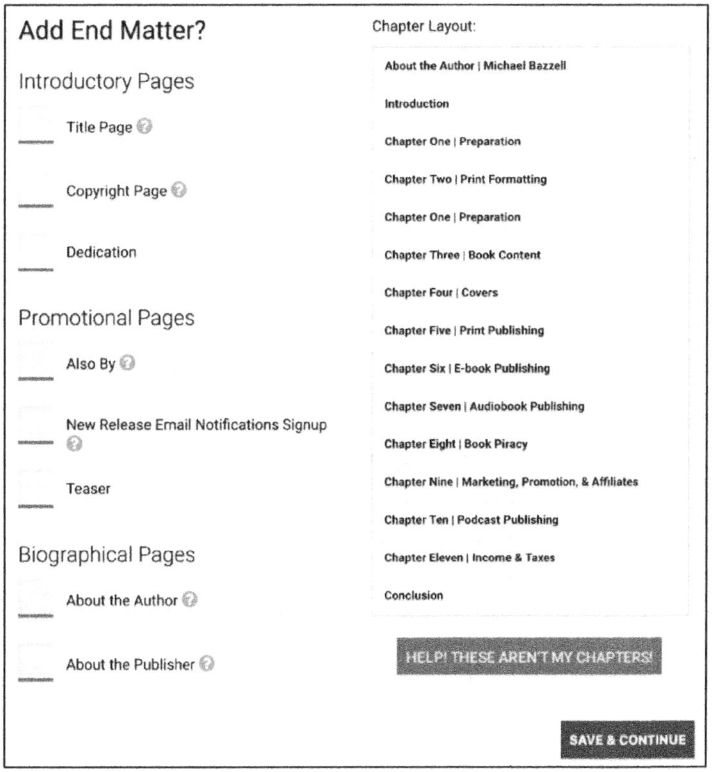

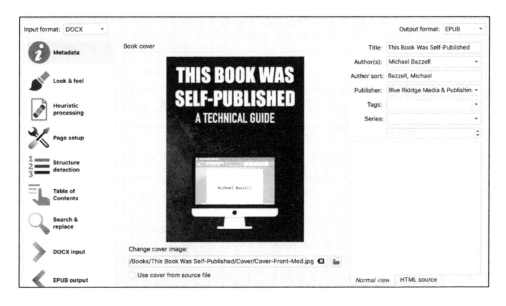

Add End Matter?
Introductory Pages
Title Page
Copyright Page
Dedication
Promotional Pages
Also By
New Release Email Notifications Signup
Teaser
Biographical Pages
About the Author
About the Publisher
Chapter Layout:
About the Author | Michael Bazzell
Introduction
Chapter One | Preparation
Chapter Two | Print Formatting
Chapter One | Preparation
Chapter Three | Book Content
Chapter Four | Covers
Chapter Five | Print Publishing
Chapter Six | E-book Publishing
Chapter Seven | Audiobook Publishing
Chapter Eight | Book Piracy
Chapter Nine | Marketing, Promotion, & Affiliates
Chapter Ten | Podcast Publishing
Chapter Eleven | Income & Taxes
Conclusion
HELP! THESE AREN'T MY CHAPTERS!
SAVE & CONTINUE

Figure 6.07: The Draft2Digital EPUB conversion process.

Input format: DOCX
Output format: EPUB
Metadata
Look & feel
Heuristic processing
Page setup
Structure detection
Table of Contents
Search & replace
DOCX input
EPUB output
Book cover
THIS BOOK WAS SELF-PUBLISHED
A TECHNICAL GUIDE
Change cover image:
/Books/This Book Was Self-Published/Cover/Cover-Front-Med.jpg
Use cover from source file
Title: This Book Was Self-Published
Author(s): Michael Bazzell
Author sort: Bazzell, Michael
Publisher: Blue Riddge Media & Publishin
Tags:
Series:
Normal view
HTML source

Figure 6.08: A Calibre conversion window.

After the conversion process completes, right-click the book and select "View" then "View specific format". Choose the EPUB option and review your book in the popup reader window. If you find any spacing issues, you will need to modify the Word file and resubmit. Since Calibre does not have the issue which Kindle Create had with the frames around text, we should not need to modify much. The frames were automatically removed during the process. To access the converted EPUB file, right-click the book and select "Open containing folder". You can copy and paste the generated EPUB file for upload to IngramSpark.

Now that we have an EPUB file suitable for publication, we can pick up where we left off with IngramSpark in the previous chapter. We had finished our print version publication process, but we were stuck on the E-book without having an EPUB file. Upload your EPUB version to your project and finish the submission process. IngramSpark distributes your book to the following.

24Symbols	De Marque Retail	LitRes eBook
Amazon	eBooks.com	LIX
Apple	Hummingbird DM	RedShelf (Virdocs)
Barnes & Noble Nook	ITSI Education UK	SpoonRead
BibliU.com	Kobo	VitalSource
Bookmate	Libreka	Wook
Booktopia	Libri	

There are two nuances with this. If your book title is already on Amazon, or has appeared on Amazon within the past 12 months, then IngramSpark will not submit another copy. This is desired by most, and the previous chapter explained how this can bring on more royalties. When people purchase your E-book on Amazon, you receive a 70% royalty. When purchased through IngramSpark, the rate is only 40%. By ensuring Amazon is the priority for Kindle sales, you make more money.

Next, IngramSpark cannot sell your E-book through Apple if your title already exists on their platform. This is also desired by most authors. When people purchase your E-book on Apple, you receive a 70% royalty. When purchased through IngramSpark, the rate is only 40%. By ensuring Apple is the priority for E-book sales on their platform, you make more money.

Are you tired of all of the options yet? I understand if you feel overwhelmed. You need to make a choice of how you want to proceed. I believe you have two considerations based on your priorities of convenience versus income.

Convenience: The easiest route is to upload your Kindle version to Amazon and your EPUB version to IngramSpark. This will make your book available to practically every E-book outlet. You will take a royalty hit on your non-Amazon sales, but you have much less work in front of you. You also have a full reporting system in one location in order to track digital sales.

Income: If you don't like the idea of IngramSpark taking 20%-30% of your royalties, you can bypass their E-book option altogether. This requires you to manually submit your book to your chosen distributors. This is not difficult, but it can be time-consuming.

What did I do? I submitted only to Amazon and IngramSpark. I chose this for a few reasons. First, E-book sales outside of Amazon are minimal for me. The extra effort of manual account creation and upload at each service was probably not worth the potential royalty income. Second, I did not want to create additional tax reporting obligations. I can provide my royalty income from Amazon and IngramSpark to my accountant and be done. Tracking down tax forms from a dozen distributors is time-consuming and can cost me more in work hours from my tax professional. If you plan to sell thousands of copies on Apple or Nook, then it may justify the numerous accounts across the platforms. The E-book price for this book on Amazon is $7.41 and my royalty is $5.00. The E-book price on all other platforms is $7.99 (IngramSpark requires prices to end in .99) and my royalty is $3.20.

Please note that you should NOT purchase the print and E-book combination from IngramSpark if you plan to manually upload your digital book(s) to each third-party service after publication. If you have the combination package, you may be required to submit both the print and digital versions during checkout. This digital publication can take priority over manual upload at a later date to each service. Choose only ONE of the following paths before you publish any E-books to non-Amazon distributors.

- Allow IngramSpark to furnish digital books to third parties.

- Upload to Apple, Barnes & Noble, and others first before publishing with IngramSpark.

- Eliminate the E-book option with IngramSpark and manually submit to third parties.

The following pages explain the process of publishing your own E-book directly through Apple, Barnes & Noble, and Kobo. These are the most popular U.S. options. You can use the lessons in these sections to replicate your work across the remaining E-book distributors if desired. In 2016, I submitted a self-published title to every option possible. To date, I have never sold a single E-book outside of Amazon, Apple, and Nook. Some authors report international sales through Kobo, but I am not seeing any.

In 2019, Amazon was the obvious leader of E-book sales. Next was Apple iBooks, NookPress by Barnes & Noble, then Kobo. Therefore, I present these options within the same order in the following pages. I have omitted Google Play Books for two reasons. First, I do not believe they have a substantial market share of purchased E-books. Second, they tend to randomly close signup to new creators, enforcing a backlist waiting period. You can research their current status of enrollment at play.google.com/books/uploads.

Apple Books Creation & Distribution

Uploading your E-book directly to Apple is only required if BOTH of the following are true.

- You want your book available through Apple Books (formerly iBooks) for viewing on iPads and other Apple devices.

- You do NOT want IngramSpark to facilitate publication on Apple Books with a royalty of 40% (versus 70% direct from Apple).

Since I have provided extreme detail regarding the publication process for E-books through KDP and IngramSpark, I will only summarize the steps for Apple, Barnes & Noble, and Kobo.

- Create an iTunes Connect Account at https://authors.apple.com/epub-upload.

- If you already possess an Apple ID, sign in when prompted.

- If you do not have an Apple ID, create one when prompted. Once registered, make sure to complete the "Payment & Shipping" section, but a credit card is not required.

- If you receive an error about your account requiring connection to an Apple device, download iTunes on either a Mac or Windows computer and sign in to your Apple account. More information about this is presented in the podcast chapter.

- Verify the confirmation email if prompted.

- Enter your banking and tax information.

Apple will review your information and approve or reject your account within 48 hours. However, you can continue the publication process while you wait. The following steps upload your EPUB file previously created into Apple's system.

- Navigate to authors.apple.com/epub-upload and click "Sign in to iTunes Connect".

- Upload your E-book cover file.

- If desired, upload a sample chapter EPUB file.

- Upload the EPUB file of your entire book previously created.

- Enter the metadata of your book including the title, subtitle, description, and author.

- Select the same book categories as previously chosen.

- Enter the desired publisher (imprint) name.

- If allowed, leave the ISBN field blank.

- If forced to provide an ISBN, supply the number issued to your E-book by IngramSpark. It is preferred to leave this blank in order to prevent conflict over royalties.

- Complete the territorial pricing section to mirror your KDP settings.

- Return to iTunes Connect and click on "My Books". It may take 48 hours to appear.

- Select the book, click "Rights & Pricing", then "Add New Countries or Regions".

- Provide the desired book pricing.

- Enable or disable DRM as you did previously with Kindle.

- Select your publication date (can be immediately).

Apple will use your book price and base currency to generate appropriate pricing for all countries and regions. Note that you must submit your E-book to Apple BEFORE digital publication through IngramSpark in order to receive the 70% Apple royalty instead of the 40% IngramSpark royalty. If you publish directly through Apple, expect to receive an IRS tax reporting form 1099-MISC if you were paid over $10.00 in royalties.

Some online statistics show that E-books purchased through Apple are more than Barnes & Noble, Kobo, and all other non-Amazon distributors combined. If you only want one additional option aside from Amazon, I believe Apple should be it. Many people consider their iPads as a dedicated E-book reading device.

Since iPads all possess color displays, consider these devices when you create your final documents. Be sure to use high-resolution color images whenever possible. This is another reason I always recommend a proper press-ready PDF created with Adobe Acrobat Pro. Using the PDF export option embedded into your operating system, such as macOS, compresses all images to 72 dpi. Most publishers, including Amazon, prefer images at 200 dpi minimum, with a recommendation of 300 dpi. While your print customers may not notice this compression, your iPad readers will.

Nook Creation & Distribution

Uploading your E-book directly to Barnes & Noble (Nook) is only required if BOTH of the following are true.

- You want your book available through Barnes & Noble for viewing on Nook devices.

- You do NOT want IngramSpark to facilitate publication on Apple Books with a royalty of 40% (versus 65% direct from Barnes & Noble).

Barnes & Noble is the company which owns Nook. While Barnes & Noble is a major company with multiple focuses, Nook Press is a subsidiary company which only specializes in self-publishing services. The term Barnes & Noble will be used synonymously with Nook. The following steps will publish your E-book on this platform.

- Navigate to press.barnesandnoble.com.

- Create a new account or log in with an existing account.

- Click on "Get Started" and select the E-book option.

- Create your project and provide the details about your book, such as the title and author.

- Upload the cover JPG and interior EPUB files.

- Allow the review process to complete, which may take 48 hours.

If you ever want to make changes to your book, do so through the account portal. You can immediately update the pricing under "Book details". Submitting a new EPUB file must go through the same review process, but your previous version will stay on sale during this time. Note that you must submit your E-book to Barnes & Noble BEFORE digital publication through IngramSpark in order to receive the 65% Barnes & Noble royalty instead of the 40% IngramSpark royalty.

As of 2019, Barnes & Noble was still making new Nook readers. However, sales of new units have steeply declined from $933 million in 2012 to $92 million in 2019. While an important consideration for global availability of your title, I would not expect sales which compare to Amazon or Apple.

Kobo Creation & Distribution

Uploading your E-book directly to Kobo is only required if BOTH of the following are true.

- You want your book available through Kobo for viewing on Kobo tablets.

- You do NOT want IngramSpark to facilitate publication on Kobo with a royalty of 40% (versus 70% direct from Kobo).

Kobo e-reader tablets are very popular in many countries and commonly sold at Walmart in the United States.

- Navigate to writinglife.kobobooks.com.

- Create an account and log in.

- Select the "eBOOKS" option.

- Click the "Create new eBook" button.

- Complete the "Describe your eBook" section with the previously used details.

- Upload your cover JPG and interior EPUB files previously created within the "Add eBook content" section.

- Mirror the rights and payment details previously discussed within the "Rights and Distribution" and "Set the price" sections.

- Set the publication date as the current date, and click "Publish your eBook".

After a quick review process, your E-book should be available for sale through Kobo. Note that you must submit your E-book to Kobo BEFORE digital publication through IngramSpark in order to receive the 70% Kobo royalty instead of the 40% IngramSpark royalty. Overall, I have not experienced many sales through this vendor. I am happy to allow IngramSpark to facilitate these minimal sales.

Free Digital File Creation & Distribution

Some authors freely distribute their E-books via the internet. This may be to build interest in the title or as part of a marketing campaign to bring in new related business. I never release my books freely in any format, but you may find this to be beneficial. You can use Calibre to convert your Word document to multiple formats. The following is a summary of each recommended file type.

- **PDF:** As explained previously, this is the universal format for desktop operating systems and mobile telephones. It is the only true representation of your final print PDF. Every other format alters your layout substantially.

- **EPUB:** This is the most universal format. It can read by practically any E-book reader, with the exception of Kindle.

- **MOBI:** These files can be read via Kindle and most mobile telephone devices.

- **AZW3:** AZW files are proprietary to Kindle and is based on the Mobi file format. They contain better compression than Mobi files.

- **TXT:** This is the most universal text format which can be read on practically any device. It displays only text and excludes all images.

Some authors provide PDF, EPUB, and Mobi files on their website in order to offer their book in formats which cover every possible device. This should only be considered if you want your book to be more popular without any additional royalties. If you decide that free distribution of your book is more advantageous to your work than selling it, be sure to offer all possible formats.

Most importantly, understand that you can never take your work back from the internet. Once your files are distributed freely online, they will be available forever. You cannot control the duplication of files across websites and personal computers. You cannot update the content when there are thousands of files on independent machines. However, modifying your content with official E-book publishers, such as KDP, applies to all future downloads of your work.

If you later identify an error in your book, such as a misspelled word, you can correct it and resubmit your work. You are not stuck with the embarrassment forever. Compare this to the days when self-published authors ordered thousands of books and stored them in the garage. There was a lot of pressure to have perfect content which would be permanently archived. Did I mention that we live in amazing times?

File Size Reduction

The previous tutorials should suffice for most self-published books. If your book possesses numerous high resolution images, you may have a problem. The final Word document for this book was over 24 megabytes in size due to numerous screen captures. That is acceptable for the print version, which should always represent the highest quality interior as possible. However, E-books of this size can be problematic. Kindle charges a "delivery fee" of $0.15 for each megabyte of file size. However, Kindle now has a great compression strategy which usually eliminates this concern. During your upload of a KPF file, KDP compresses the images in order to minimize the delivery fee. The fee for this book was only $0.27 after default compression.

No other self-publishing E-book service charges a delivery fee. However, you may wish to minimize the file size of your book before creating an EPUB or PDF version. Only apply these actions if you know they are needed! Most readers should not need to take these steps. I conducted the following steps as a test with my own content, but the final compressed file was not needed or used during the publication of my E-book.

- Open the current master document within Word and save it as "Interior-Ebook.docx". Never modify the document used for the print version, always make a new copy.

- If on a Mac computer within Word, compress all images to 220 ppi and remove cropped areas by clicking "File" then "Reduce File Size". Select "220 ppi" and "Delete cropped areas of picture". Click "OK" and save the document.

- If on a Windows computer within Word, compress all images to 220 ppi and remove cropped areas by clicking the "Picture Format" tab, "Adjust" group, and "Compress Pictures" option. In the new windows de-select "Apply only to this picture" and select "220 ppi". Click "OK" and save the document.

- Check the new file size. If still too large, repeat the process choosing 150 ppi.

With this book, the size at 220 ppi was 20 megabytes while the size at 150 ppi dropped to 11 megabytes. If necessary, you could review all of your images and locate those which are very large, redundant, or not essential to the book. You could then remove them from the E-book document, which will also minimize the file size. I want to stress again that most readers should not need this size reduction strategy. Allow KDP and the EPUB conversion options to compress the images as programmed. However, know that you can control file size before executing alternative delivery methods with documents such as PDF, EPUB, and Mobi.

What did I do? I made a copy of my Word file and removed the Table of Contents and Index. I then uploaded that to Draft2Digital and exported an EPUB file. The file was almost perfect, but needed some spacing changes. I imported the EPUB into Calibre and made some slight modifications using the "Edit Book" option when right-clicking on the file. This required some basic knowledge of HTML coding which is beyond the scope of this book. I then saved the EPUB and imported it into both KDP and IngramSpark. I did not use Kindle Create at all for my digital version. However, I believe it is the best option for first-time digital authors. If you are tech-savvy, you might consider using the Draft2Digital and Calibre combination. In my experience, Draft2Digital converts Word documents into EPUB files better than Kindle Create converts Word documents into KFX files. Plus, the EPUB can be used for all digital uploads. However, Kindle Create is much more user-friendly.

E-book Publishing Checklist

- Understand the benefits and risks of publishing PDF files.

- Download and install Kindle Create.

- Create your Kindle version E-book.

- Test the Kindle version on all reader types.

- Check for page and paragraph spacing.

- Enroll or exclude Amazon-exclusive programs.

- Choose your E-book pricing strategy.

- Conduct a free book promotion, if desired.

- Create an E-book project at IngramSpark, if desired.

- Convert your Word file to EPUB.

- Upload the EPUB file to IngramSpark and choose distribution options.

- Consider third-party distribution directly through Apple, Nook, and Kobo.

- If necessary, compress images in order to reduce file size.

CHAPTER SEVEN
AUDIOBOOK PUBLISHING

A 2019 study by the Pew Research Center reports that 72% of adults in the U.S. say they have read a book in the past 12 months. Print books remain the most popular format for reading, with 65% of adults saying they had read a print book in the year before the survey. These stats are relatively unchanged from prior years, but audiobook listeners have grown. The same study reports that 20% of adults in the U.S. have listened to an audiobook within the past year. The Audio Publishers Association reported $1.2 billion in audiobook revenue from 2019, up 16% from the previous year. Does this news increase your interest in audiobook publishing? The process is likely easier than you think and can be done yourself without professional help.

I confess I have never released audiobooks of my previous titles. However, I have assisted others with creating their own audiobook product. Although I publish a weekly podcast in my own voice, I am not confident people want to hear me read this book. However, that is not the reason I do not plan on creating an audiobook version of this title. Most audiobook guidance websites agree that reference books do not make good audiobooks. Reading a list of appropriate print book dimensions or verbally explaining the nuances of Photoshop without the ability to display images sounds like a nightmare. I assume people want to read and revisit printed text whenever they start their journey into self-publishing. I doubt anyone wants to search for a section of audio in which I explain a specific problem.

Audiobooks work best with fiction or biographies. If you have written a book which delivers a story, an audiobook may be in your future. Fortunately, there is a single service called Audiobook Creation Exchange (ACX) which distributes audiobooks to Audible, Amazon, and iTunes. ACX is owned by Audible, which is an Amazon company. The partnership with Apple is surprising, but it really makes the entire process of complete distribution easy. Let's walk through the process together.

First, you must decide on the narrator for your audiobook. You can hire people through ACX which will do all of the hard work for you, but this comes at a cost. A 50,000 word book can cost $1,000 to $2,000 in narration fees. This book would cost more than $2,500. Most self-published authors tackle the narration themselves. What better voice than the author's? This chapter will assume you want to narrate your own book.

First, let's create an account at ACX with the following steps.

- Sign in to an Amazon or KDP account and navigate to www.acx.com/account/new.

- Complete the registration forms and click "Save".

- Navigate to www.acx.com/settings and complete the "Tax Information" and "Bank Information" sections. Even though this is an Amazon company, you will need to replicate the information previously supplied to KDP.

- Click "Add your title" in the upper-right.

- Choose the print version of your book. The results displayed are titles associated with your name as the author. If your book is not visible, you will need to contact customer support.

- In the pop-up window, choose the "I already have audio files…" option.

- Select the "World" territory.

- Select the exclusive 40% royalty option and appropriate language.

- Read and agree to the terms of service.

- Complete the "Title Details" page and click "Continue".

- Enter the chapter details similar to my book as follows.
    About the Author
    Introduction
    Chapter 1: Preparation
    Chapter 2: Print Formatting

- After adding all chapters, click "Save and Continue".

You are now ready to upload the audio files for your audiobook. Before you create these files, please consider the following audio requirements. I will explain each.

- **Consistent in overall sound and formatting:** Consistency in audio levels, tone, noise level, spacing, and pronunciation gives the listener an enjoyable experience. Drastic changes can be jarring to the listener and are not reflective of a professional production. This distracts from the listening experience and may lead to poor reviews and reduced sales.

- **Comprised of all mono or all stereo files:** Submitted audiobooks may not contain both mono and stereo files. Mono files are strongly recommended. Before being added to the various audio bookstores, submitted files are encoded in a variety of formats which listeners have the option of downloading. Titles submitted with both stereo and mono files will cause errors during this encoding process and the title's release may be delayed.

- **Include opening and closing credits:** The opening credits must contain the name of the audiobook, the name of the author(s), and the name of the narrator(s). Closing credits must, at minimum, state "the end". These opening credits help listeners confirm what they are about to hear, and that they are listening to the start of the desired audiobook. Closing credits confirm to the listener they have reached the end.

- **Include a retail sample:** The retail audio sample used on Audible and Amazon is a short preview of your Audiobook. Apple's iTunes automatically uses the first five minutes of the book as their sample. Pick a strong sample which catches the potential listener and encourages them to buy your audiobook. The sample must start with narration and not credits or music. It must not contain any explicit material and should be anywhere from one to five minutes in length. Most authors use the beginning of their book as the sample.

- **Be recorded by a human:** Text-to-speech or other automated recordings are not allowed. Listeners choose audiobooks for the performance of the material as well as the story. To meet that expectation, your audiobook must be recorded by a human.

- **192 kbps or higher MP3s:** Titles are encoded in a variety of formats that customers have the option of downloading. 192 kbps (or higher) Constant Bit Rate MP3 files are required so this encoding process works without error. You may upload 256 kbps or 320 kbps files if you'd like, but the difference in quality heard by listeners will be negligible.

- **Contain only one chapter or section per file:** Each audio file must contain an entire section or chapter, and none can be over 120 minutes. This ensures listeners can easily navigate between sections and that skipping forwards or backwards moves them forward or back one section or chapter. Both the opening credits and closing credits must be separate files.

- **Section header must be read aloud:** These announcements help the listener understand what section of the book they are listening to without having to look at their player.

- **Have room tone at the head and at the tail:** Room tone is the background noise in a room. For audiobook purposes, room tone should be the resting sound in your studio and as close to silent as possible. Each file must have 0.5 to 1 second of room tone at its beginning and 1 to 5 seconds of room tone at its end. This space is required to ensure titles are successfully encoded in the many formats made available to customers. It also gives listeners an audio cue that they have reached the beginning or end of a section.

- **Be free of extraneous sounds:** Extraneous sounds such as mic pops, mouse clicks, or excessive mouth noise can distract listeners from the story.

- **Measure between -23dB and -18dB RMS:** Root Mean Square (RMS) is a conventional way to measure the effective average value of an audio signal as well as the perceived dynamic range values of that signal. Each file needs to fall between the specific volume range of -23dB and -18dB RMS. By keeping all files within this range, not too loud and not too soft, listeners won't have to constantly adjust the volume of their playback device.

- **Have -3dB peak values:** By manipulating the peak audio, you will reduce the possibility of distortion, which can seriously reduce the quality of the listening experience.

- **Have a maximum -60dB noise floor:** The noise floor is the level of the noise below the audio signal in decibels (dB). This is generally considered to be the audible level of background noise in a recording, where no narration is taking place. It is important to ensure your files have a noise floor no higher than -60dB RMS. Noisy files that contain background sounds and other distractions make it difficult for listeners to focus on the material.

This may sound overwhelming, and it can be. However, I will tackle all of the requirements as I create audio files throughout this chapter. I assume at this point that you are ready to record your own voice reading your book. Once you have your ACX account ready, it is time to record your first file. First consider the following in reference to your vocal capture.

- **Microphone:** I recommend a USB microphone with condenser, specifically the Yeti made by Blue. If you are on a tight budget, I have also used the Snowball made by Blue. The Yeti can be found for $100 while the Snowball is commonly sold for under $50. I never recommend headset earbud-style microphones or embedded mics within devices such as a laptop or mobile device. My Yeti is always in the "Cardiod" setting, which can be controlled by the knob on the back. This mode records sound sources which are directly in front of the microphone.

- **Environment:** I doubt many readers possess an isolated sound booth for perfect vocal capture. If you have a decent microphone, a dedicated small sound-proof area is not vital. I record in my home office with good results. If you want to create a better recording, consider capturing your audio from within a closet. If that is overkill for your needs, draping a blanket around your back and sides can have a huge impact. Most importantly, eliminate any background noise such as appliances, pets, toilets, and music.

Now that you have your vocal recording area ready, you need some software which will convert your voice into a digital file. There are countless audio recording software suites which range from minimalistic apps to expensive professional options. If you are already familiar with something common, such as Garage Band, then you should use that. If you have no experience with digital audio recording, I recommend Audacity (audacityteam.org). This free software can be installed on Windows, Mac, or Linux and provides all of the basic features we need without excess bells and whistles. This doesn't mean that the software is self-explanatory; there will still be a learning curve. However, I will provide some guidance on the basics.

Hardware Detection: Make sure your microphone is connected and recognized by your operating system before launching Audacity. Open the system settings for Windows or Mac and make sure the input volume is maximized for the microphone.

Hardware Selection: Within Audacity, choose your microphone from the top input entries, as seen in Figure 7.01. If supported, always choose a stereo recording.

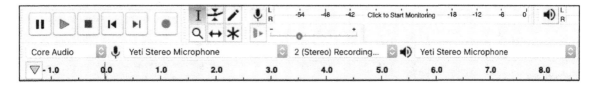

Figure 7.01: The Audacity hardware selection menus.

Track Creation: Within Audacity, we need to add a new track, which will capture your voice. In the Audacity file menu, select "Tracks", "Add New", then "Mono Track". This will create a new entry within your software.

Audio Recording: Click the red circle to begin your recording. Ensure that you see the visual representation of captured audio, as seen in Figure 7.02. The black square will stop the recording. As long as your cursor is placed at the end of any track, the red circle will begin recording at the designated location. If you place the cursor within previously recorded audio, it will record at that chosen place. This can risk losing or overwriting audio, so use caution.

Figure 7.02: A recorded audio track.

Edit Your Audio Files

Your recorded chapters are not ready for upload. They would almost certainly be rejected. We must process each file in a similar way in order to have consistency. I recommend recording all of your files before editing any of them. Try to match the overall audio level. Record all of the files in the same location, at the same time of the day, with your face the same distance from the microphone. After your recording is complete, consider the following editing tasks.

Content Removal: When you record your sections and chapters, never stop recording. Even if you need to pause to gather your thoughts or take a drink, let the recording go. My Yeti microphone provides a physical mute button which is beneficial for visually identifying portions of my audio without sound. When finished, I can select any silent areas by dragging the cursor throughout them, and click the delete key on the keyboard. When mastered, no one will suspect your chapter was not created perfectly within one take. Figure 7.03 displays a selection of silence for removal. If you need to zoom in to see the file better, use the "View" and "Zoom" options.

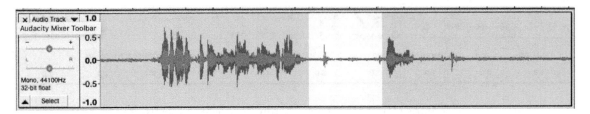

Figure 7.03: Selection of silence within Audacity for removal.

Sound Amplification: Most vocal recordings are "quiet" and need amplified. I typically need to amplify my recordings by 2.0-6.0 decibels. If you need to boost your recording, double click the audio wave within a track in order to select the entire recording. Then click on "Effect" in the menu and choose "Amplify". Set your desired level, such as 2.0 to 3.0, and click "OK". Figure 7.04 displays my enhanced audio file. While it may appear visually similar to the previous image, the overall volume is higher. I encourage you to play this file while playing a professionally-created audiobook in your browser. Which is louder? Depending on your microphone and environment, you may need to boost your audio levels more. Once you reach a volume which is close to the professional audiobooks, we can remember this setting for future usage.

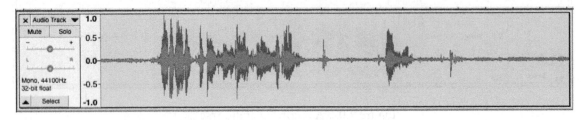

Figure 7.04: An amplified Audacity audio track.

Sound Limiting: If you amplified your track, you may have a few places where the audio is too "hot" and exceeds the threshold which prevents "clipping". I typically conduct a hard limit to the entire audio file to make sure there are no undesired loud portions. In the Audacity menu, click "Effect" then "Limiter". Choose "Hard Limit" in the menu and change the "Limit to (dB)" field to "-3.00". This will make sure no portions of your audio are too close to the maximum decibels required by ACX. Figure 7.05 displays this menu while Figure 7.06 displays my audio file result.

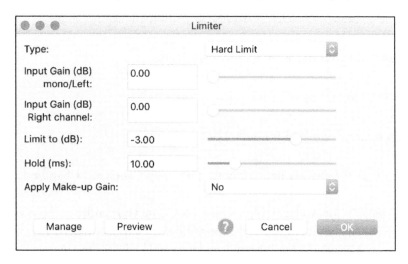

Figure 7.05: An Audacity hard limiter dialogue.

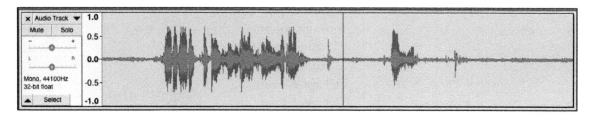

Figure 7.06: An audio file after hard limiting to ACX specifications.

Take a moment to compare Figures 7.04 and 7.06. The content is identical, but the files are quite different. The first spike of audio "touches" the top of the track boundaries in Figure 7.04. After we applied the hard limiting in Figure 7.06, you can see that this spike is much lower. It is now within an acceptable range, as identified by ACX. This single modification may be the difference between your audiobook being accepted or rejected.

Archive Your Audio Files

It is important to save your project as you record. I recommend creating a new Audacity project for each section or chapter. For each section or chapter, conduct the following within a new instance of Audacity.

- Click "File", "New", "Tracks", "Add New", and then "Mono Track".

- Record and edit your file as previously explained.

- Click "File", "Save Project", then "Save Project As".

- Choose a folder designated for audiobook recording.

- Save the file as the chapter name followed by ".aup", such as "Chapter-1.aup".

AUP is the file extension for Audacity files. These files store your entire audio project, but cannot be uploaded to ACX. In a moment, we will export these files appropriately. If I had recorded this book, my folder would be titled "Audiobook", and it would be inside my master folder tilted "This Book Is Self-Published", as previously explained. My list of files would appear as the following.

Author.aup
Introduction.aup
Chapter-1.aup
Chapter-2.aup
Chapter-3.aup
Chapter-4.aup
Chapter-5.aup
Chapter-6.aup
Chapter-7.aup
Chapter-8.aup
Chapter-9.aup
Chapter-10.aup
Chapter-11.aup
Conclusion.aup

Export Your Audio Files

Once your audio files are recorded, edited and ready for publication, you must export them in the appropriate format for ACX. Open each section or chapter AUP file and conduct the following within Audacity.

- Click "File", "Export", and then "Export as MP3".

- Change the "Bit Rate Mode" to "Constant".

- Choose a quality of "192 kbps".

- Change the "Channel Mode" to "Force export to mono".

- Choose the appropriate storage location and click "Save".

- Within the "Metadata tags" window, click "Clear" then "OK".

Figure 7.07 displays my options, which saves the MP3 file in the appropriate format within my Audiobook folder.

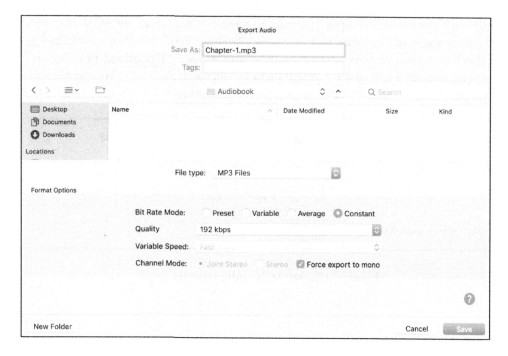

Figure 7.07: The MP3 export options within Audacity.

Submit Your Audio Files

After your audio files for your audiobook are recorded, edited, and exported, you can now upload them to ACX for review. Conduct the following within a web browser.

- Navigate to www.acx.com/dashboard and click the "In Production" link.

- Click "Upload Audiobook" next to your desired title.

- Click the "Browse" button next to each of your sections or chapters and upload the associated MP3 file for that section.

- Allow the service to analyze the audio.

- Repeat the process for each section or chapter.

- When finished, click the "I'm Done" button.

It is likely that ACX will find a problem with your project. The most common issues include small cover art, missing segments, and inappropriate room tone at the head and tail of the audio files. Be sure to understand the requirements previously explained before recording anything. Keep working through the process and pay attention to any alerts presented by ACX. If the file did not pass analysis, you should see a link to the "Audio Analysis Tab", which is visible in Figure 7.08. Clicking this link should present a new page which includes a "Download Full Report" button. This option downloads a spreadsheet which includes details of all errors. My test file included the content visible in Figure 7.09. It identifies my RMS as too low.

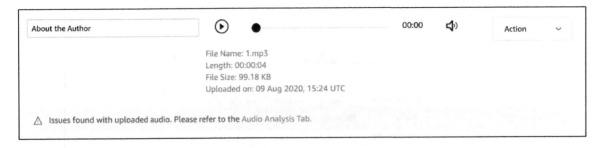

Figure 7.08: An ACX audio analysis error.

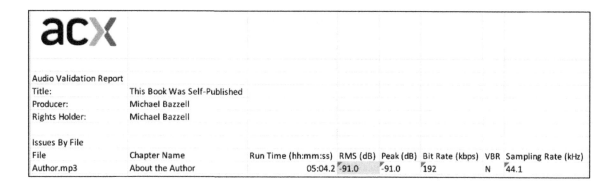

Figure 7.09: An ACX error report spreadsheet.

After all of your audio files are analyzed and accepted, you can submit for publication. This step is usually approved within 48 hours, and you will see the audio version of your book available on Amazon, Audible, and Apple.

I cannot stress enough the simplification of this chapter. Narrating audiobooks is tough work, and the editing process is crucial. If any file does not meet the requirements of ACX, you are stuck until that situation is corrected. KDP printed books have general submission requirements, but these are fairly forgiving and a poorly formatted book can slide through the automated checks. E-books possess even less scrutiny which is why we see so many improperly formatted titles floating around. Audiobooks are the exception. Your audio version will require a lot of time and frustration. However, the final result can be quite rewarding.

Audiobook Publishing Checklist

- Consider the benefits of an audiobook.

- Create an account with ACX.

- Understand the audio file requirements.

- Configure the appropriate microphone and software applications.

- Record your audiobook.

- Edit your files for sound amplification and limiting.

- Archive your files.

- Export audio files to properly-encoded MP3 versions.

- Submit your files to ACX for analysis.

- Publish your audiobook.

CHAPTER EIGHT
BOOK PIRACY

It is extremely likely that someone will post your book online without your consent and make it freely available to anyone with an internet connection. If this happens, it is possible that hundreds or thousands of people will download your book from a free source instead of purchasing through official channels. You will lose many sales, and there is very little you can do about it once your title is out in the wild. This is called book piracy, and it is a huge problem. This chapter is dedicated to identifying, minimizing, embracing, and monitoring the piracy of your work. I will pull from my own experiences with my own stolen titles and offer some steps you can take before and after a title has appeared online without your permission.

We should first understand the ways in which your work goes from a legitimate online purchase option to a free download from an unofficial website. There are three ways this is likely to happen.

Kindle Version: If you released your work as a Kindle digital version, it will typically appear online very quickly, especially if you offer it as a free read through Kindle Unlimited. Someone will download the free or paid version through Amazon, usually directly to a computer. If it was downloaded onto a Kindle device, the file can be copied to a computer via USB cable. This file possesses Digital Rights Management (DRM) protection, which requires a specific Kindle device in order to be viewed. Copying this file to another Kindle does not work. Therefore, the user must remove the DRM using one of multiple software options such as DeDRM, Epubor, and others. For obvious reasons, I will not explain the DRM removal process here. Once a file without DRM is created, it can be uploaded to numerous book piracy websites and shared freely. The file will open within any E-book reader.

Print Version: Refusing to release a digital version of your book does not remove the threat of book piracy. The abundance of affordable sheet-fed scanners can turn your printed work into a PDF within minutes. Typically, a person reads your work and decides it should be shared with the world for free. The pages are cut from the spine and inserted into a scanner or copy machine. The software for the machine scans both sides of each page and assembles the entire work into a single PDF file. These are typically poor quality and large files, but still usable. The PDF can be uploaded to various book piracy websites in a universal format which can be read on any device or computer.

DRM-Free Digital Version: If you have released a PDF, EPUB, or Mobi file without any protection, then your file can be shared with ease. These files are typically very small and represent the best quality possible. These are always preferred within the book piracy community.

You should decide right away whether you have concerns about free copies of your book being shared or want to embrace the activity. While you cannot completely prevent book piracy, you can minimize or delay the sharing of your work. Some people believe that book piracy leads to more sales due to the free advertisement and word of mouth. However, I disagree. Once your book can be downloaded easily, most people will go the free route instead of through an official purchase. There will still be a number of readers who insist on a legitimate purchase, but I believe those numbers are constantly decreasing. Consider my own experiences as follows.

- On January 1, 2016, I released a print-only third edition of my book *Hiding From The Internet*. Sales were continuously strong each month. On April 1, 2016, I released a Kindle edition of this title. Digital sales were strong from April 1, 2016 through April 15, 2016. On April 12, 2016, a free digital version of this book was released to twelve different book piracy websites. After this, digital sales dropped by 60% while print sales dropped by 40%. I can never prove the correlation of these sales to book piracy, but I feel confident there was a negative impact.

- On January 26, 2018, I released a print-only sixth edition of my book *Open Source Intelligence Techniques*. Sales were continuously strong each month for the entire year. I never released a digital edition of this title in order to avoid or delay piracy. In March of 2019, a free scanned PDF of this book was released by the Internet Archive at archive.org. They had obtained a physical copy, scanned it, and offered it as an official digital release within their online library. I contested this action, and they removed it within a week.

- On April 2, 2019, I was notified that this same sixth edition of my book *Open Source Intelligence Techniques* had been posted to the most popular book piracy website called Library Genesis. The PDF was identical to the file previously shared by the Internet Archive. That original scan, which they believe was legal and justified, has resulted in thousands of free copies being shared throughout the internet. After this, print sales dropped by 80%.

- On October 25, 2019, I release a print-only seventh edition of my book *Open Source Intelligence Techniques*. Sales were continuously strong each month, as expected based on previous editions. I never released a digital edition of this title in order to avoid or delay piracy. As I write this section in July of 2020, I was notified that a free scanned PDF of this book was released on a newer book piracy site called Sanet.st. I do not have any statistics to share yet, but I suspect print sales will decline.

I have learned a lot about book piracy over the past decade. I have seen a total of seven titles shared publicly on the internet and now accept this as the reality of book publishing today. I still consider print-only releases a deterrent toward book piracy. I see a substantial delay from the publishing date until someone destroys their copy and scans all of the pages. However, digital editions continue to get posted almost immediately after release. If you are a first-time publisher without an online presence, none of this may matter. If you have a large following of tech-savvy people, then expect to see copies online. Never let book piracy prevent you from creating your work, but know the risks before making your publishing decisions.

Once your work is published, you may want to monitor your title to identify unofficial downloads within the book piracy community. I present the following collection of resources. Each option presents two links. The first is the main page of the piracy resource and the second is a direct link which would search for this book. You can create your own custom links for your title; save the links as bookmarks; and check them occasionally without the need to search the title within each page. I present these in order of most popular to least.

Library Genesis:
http://gen.lib.rus.ec
http://gen.lib.rus.ec/search.php?req=this+book+was+self-published

ZLibrary:
https://b-ok.cc/
https://b-ok.cc/s/this book was self-published

Mobilism:
https://forum.mobilism.org/
https://forum.mobilism.org/search.php?keywords=this+book+was+self-published

Pirate Bay:
https://thepiratebay.org
https://thepiratebay.org/search.php?q=this+book+was+self-published

Internet Archive:
https://archive.org
https://archive.org/search.php?query=this+book+was+self-published

Internet Archive Books:
https://archive.org/details/books
https://archive.org/details/books?and[]=this+book+was+self-published

Internet Archive Texts:
https://archive.org/details/texts
https://archive.org/details/texts?and[]=this+book+was+self-published

Sanet:
https://sanet.st/
https://sanet.st/search/?q=this+book+was+self-published

If you locate your work on a book piracy website, you may be able to have it removed. While some sites, such as Library Genesis ignore removal requests, others honor them. Most sites allow a removal request under the laws of the Digital Millennium Copyright Act of 1998 (DMCA). This is basically an opportunity to disclose that a website is in possession of work which you hold a copyright claim. This is typically a formality, and your options are as follows.

Library Genesis: This service does not honor removal requests.

ZLibrary: This service allows removal requests under DMCA with all details available on their DMCA page located at https://b-ok.cc/dmca.php. However, they seldom honor the request. I sent the email visible in Figure 8.01 to the DMCA address of support@bookmail.org.

I respectfully request that the following titles be removed from b-ok.cc and any other sites in your control:

https://b-ok.cc/book/5275683/321b05
https://b-ok.cc/book/4885701/51cc0c
https://b-ok.cc/book/3312960/f6b090
https://b-ok.cc/book/5411774/0e3c62
https://b-ok.cc/book/5411773/8e76a8

I am the author and sole copyright owner of these titles. Please accept my digital signature and contact details below. I "in good faith believes that use of the material in the manner complained of is not authorized by the copyright owner, its agent, or law". The "information in the notification is accurate", and "under penalty of perjury, the complaining party is authorized to act on behalf of the owner of an exclusive right that is allegedly infringed".

My Amazon book page, which includes these titles is available at:
https://www.amazon.com/Michael-Bazzell/e/B007GNUI92

Michael Bazzell
[email redacted]

Figure 8.01: A DMCA removal email request.

Mobilism: This service responds to DMCA requests, but only if your work is hosted with the domain or linked within the website. If someone posted links to your book which are hosted on another server, Mobilism will not remove the actual content. However, they will remove the pages which link to the downloads of your work. Their DMCA page on their website, located at https://forum.mobilism.org/ppcw.php?mode=policies&type=copyright, contains all required details. I submitted the email visible in Figure 8.02 to copyright@mobilism.org.

I respectfully request that the following pages, which each link to download files of my copyright work, be removed from Mobilism:

https://forum.mobilism.org/viewtopic.php?f=892&t=3448611&hilit=michael+bazzell
https://forum.mobilism.org/viewtopic.php?f=892&t=1664220&hilit=michael+bazzell
https://forum.mobilism.org/viewtopic.php?f=892&t=1495605&hilit=michael+bazzell

I am the author and sole copyright owner of these titles. Please accept my digital signature and contact details below. "I have a good faith belief that use of the copyrighted materials described above as allegedly infringing is not authorized by the copyright owner, its agent, or the law. I swear, under penalty of perjury, that the information in the notification is accurate and that I am the copyright owner or am authorized to act on behalf of the owner of an exclusive right that is allegedly infringed."

My Amazon book page, which includes these, titles is available at:

https://www.amazon.com/Michael-Bazzell/e/B007GNUI92

Michael Bazzell
[email redacted]

Figure 8.02: A DMCA removal email request.

Pirate Bay: This service does not honor removal requests.

Internet Archive: This service allows book removal requests under DMCA. I sent the email visible in Figure 8.03 to the DMCA address of info@archive.org.

Sanet: This service allows removal requests under DMCA with all details available on their DMCA page located at https://sanet.st/dmca/. I completed their online contact form, identifying the location (page) of the infringing content.

These requests were sent on July 20, 2020. I received the following responses.

- **ZLibrary:** No response, but the download links were removed on August 1, 2020.

- **Mobilism:** No response, but the content was removed on July 27, 2020.

- **Internet Archive:** I received an email within 24 hours confirming removal of content.

- **Sanet:** No response, but the content was removed within 24 hours.

I respectfully request that the following book, which is a digital download of work which I hold a copyright, be removed from the Internet Archive:

https://archive.org/details/opensourceintelligencetechniques

I am the author and sole copyright owner of these titles. Please accept my digital signature and contact details below. "I have a good faith belief that use of the copyrighted materials described above as allegedly infringing is not authorized by the copyright owner, its agent, or the law. I swear, under penalty of perjury, that the information in the notification is accurate and that I am the copyright owner or am authorized to act on behalf of the owner of an exclusive right that is allegedly infringed."

My Amazon book page, which includes these, titles is available at:

https://www.amazon.com/Michael-Bazzell/e/B007GNUI92

Michael Bazzell
[email redacted]

Figure 8.03: A DMCA removal email request.

Removing content is never a final solution. Once the data is in the wild, it will likely be reposted again. It is a constant game of cat-and-mouse. However, anything you can do to make it more difficult for people to download your book through free illegitimate channels increases the potential for legitimate sales. There are hundreds of book piracy websites, and I only listed the most common. You should occasionally conduct a search of your book title on Google in hopes of finding new infringement. For this book, I will be monitoring the following search queries, including the quotation marks.

- "this book was self-published" "epub"

- "this book was self-published" "pdf"

- "this book was self-published" "mobi"

- "this book was self-published" "download"

I placed the title within quotation marks in order to focus only on sites which possess the entire title and not just those words in random order. Including "epub", "pdf", and "mobi" helps me eliminate official sales channels such as Amazon. Finally, the "download" option may pick up any sites which offer an option to retrieve other formats of the book such as docx, azw, and others. You will probably encounter numerous websites which claim to possess a copy of your book available for download. However, many of these are traps to convince people to sign up for surveys and internet sales offers. If you ever encounter a site which displays a download link for your title, and you are presented with either a "loading" page or a demand to "complete one of these offers", it is usually a bogus site which does not actually possess your content.

Book piracy is annoying, but it is not the end of the world. I recommend that most authors release a digital edition of their work, knowing that free copies will be posted online. The potential sales of E-books could outweigh the concern of free copies in the wild. If you truly want to deter the spread of pirated copies of your work, consider limiting publication to KDP print services without Expanded Distribution. If you simply want your book to be read by as many people as possible, with no concerns about legitimate sales or royalties, you could consider uploading your own pirated copy to these sites.

Book Piracy Checklist

- Understand the potential for piracy of your E-book.

- Monitor your title within the most popular E-book sharing sites.

- Submit DMCA removal requests if necessary.

- Monitor search terms relative to your book.

CHAPTER NINE
MARKETING, PROMOTION, & AFFILIATES

Now that your book is available to the public, the sales should just fly in, right? I wish it were that easy. The reality is that no one may find your book without some guidance. As a self-published author, there is no company or agent arranging TV interviews or book signings. Any marketing is solely your responsibility. This can have many benefits since you are in complete control. However, the effort required by you can be substantial. Let's take a look at some basic strategies, the first of which may strike a nerve.

Please resist becoming a self-established "Best-Seller". The term is overused in practically every genre and has become meaningless. When I was searching through various authors who offer books about self-publishing, I noticed all of them were self-proclaimed "best-selling authors". What does that mean today? In previous decades, books and authors were certified as best-sellers through reputable sources such as The New York Times. Today, a few seconds of presence on an Amazon "Top 100" style of list encourages authors to announce their new status. I believe this is a mistake.

The truth is that anyone can be a best-seller today. If your book sells five copies within a few minutes, it is likely to temporarily appear within some niche category as the "Best" selling item on that page (which no one will see). Broadcasting this success to the world can be viewed as self-serving and desperate. Readers likely don't care, and no one will buy your book based on this declaration. Most people know that Amazon hands out these status symbols as if they were candy. Figure 9.01 displays an Amazon listing announcing one of my books to be a "Best Seller". For a few minutes, it was the number one selling item within the "Internet & Telecommunications" section of Amazon. The number two best seller in this same category was a blank book which you could use to document your passwords. In other words, my book was slightly better than a book without words. Worse, the password book took over the number one slot a few days later.

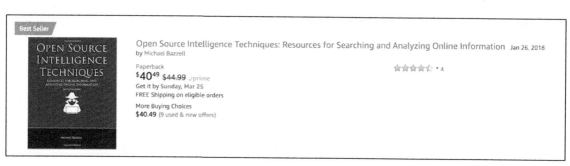

Figure 9.01: A practically meaningless Amazon "Best Seller" rating.

Promotional Images

While Amazon will display an icon of your book cover within the purchase page, this image is low quality and not appropriate for your own promotion. Anytime you post about your book on social networks or blogs, you should display a crisp and clear graphic file. I recommend having a few options available at all times. I typically create a large front cover, small front cover, and 3D cover. Let's start with the basic front cover files.

- Within your Photoshop trial, open your cover document and save the file as "Cover-Front.psd".

- Click the "Crop Tool" in the left menu, fifth option from the top.

- Drag the "slider" from the left edge toward the right, creating a crop of just the front cover. Adjust the top, bottom, left and right sliders until your cover is cropped as desired.

- Click the checkmark at the top in order to lock in the settings.

- Click "File", "Export", and "Quick Export as PNG" in the Photoshop menu.

- Save the file as "Cover-Front.png".

- Click "File", "Export", and "Export as" in the Photoshop menu.

- In the "Image Size" area, change the width to "250" and click "Export".

- Save the file as "Cover-Front-small.png".

The first file is high resolution and appropriate for any usage which requests a large file. The second file is more appropriate for social networks, email messages, newsletters, and other online advertisement. Figure 9.02 (left) displays the flat front cover image. Next, let's spice things up and create a 3D rendering.

- Navigate to https://diybookcovers.com/3Dmockups.

- Click your desired cover template and click "Next".

- Click "Browse", select the "Cover-Front.png" file, and click "Upload".

- Click "Next", "PNG", then save the file. Figure 9.02 (right) displays my project.

Figure 9.02: A flat cover promotional image (left) and 3D rendering (right).

I prefer the 3D view for most promotion. It conveys an unmistakable image of a book, and catches the eye better than a flat image. Figure 9.03 displays my own website with a different title in 3D view. I will use this format for all social network promotion.

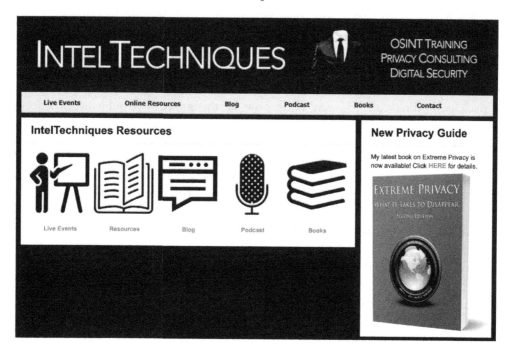

Figure 9.03: A website displaying a 3D book cover.

Websites & Blogs

I believe every author should possess some type of website. If you do not want to learn the elements of web hosting, domain registration, blog installation, HTML editing, and DNS configuration, you could consider a free blog at WordPress. If you already know how to create and host your own site, you do not need the instruction within this section. If you want a simple and free solution, even if temporary, I believe WordPress is the best way to go. Conduct the following to get started.

- Navigate to https://wordpress.com and click "Start your website".

- Enter your email address, desired username, and desired password.

- Click "Create your account". This should forward you to a domain selection page.

- Enter the title of your book without spaces. This will be used as part of the website address. I entered "thisbookwasselfpublished".

- Look for the completely free option near the top of the results portion of the page. My result appeared as "thisbookwasselfpublished.wordpress.com".

- Click "Select" next to the entry, then "Start with a free site" on the following page.

- Click the activation link sent within the confirmation email.

You now have a free WordPress website/blog without any obligation to purchase additional service packages. Mine can be seen right now at thisbookwasselfpublished.wordpress.com. However, your site has no content. Let's fix that. On the home page of your WordPress portal, add any desired information to your page. I provided a title, tagline, and then clicked "Launch site". This prompted me with attempts to sell me a custom domain, which I skipped. I had to confirm again that I wanted the free site. This made my blog public, but there was still no content showing. I conducted the following within my WordPress portal for demonstration purposes.

- Click on "Design" then "Themes" from the left menu.

- Select "Barnsbury" as the default theme and click "Edit homepage".

- Remove any undesired blocks with the "three dots" menu option within each.

- Edit text blocks as desired.

- Replace images as desired with the promotional images previously created.

- Add purchase link forwarding to affiliate URL of book on Amazon.

- Click "My Home" on the left menu and then "Edit Menus" in the right area.

- Click "Primary", then edit, add, or remove menu items.

- Add, edit, or remove social network links as desired.

- Modify the contact page as desired.

You can see this site live at https://thisbookwasselfpublished.wordpress.com and in Figure 9.04. Notice the 3D book cover, purchase link, Twitter link, and Contact page. These are the staples that allow people to identify and purchase your book, with options to follow you on Twitter or contact you directly via your site. I kept the previous background in order to see the contrast in colors. The contact page includes a form which generates an email to you within the WordPress environment. You will not need to announce your email address, and I always recommend eliminating any addresses on your site. Otherwise, expect spam to start building up in your inbox.

This WordPress page can be linked within social network posts, email messages, or any other type of marketing strategy. Search engines will eventually index the site and make it available on sites such as Google. I should disclose that I do not use this WordPress site for anything other than this demonstration, and it is far from complete. If it were going to be my primary website, I would put much more time into it and make it more robust. Since I use my own website for all of my projects, the only book promotion I publish is at https://inteltechniques.com/books.html.

Figure 9.04: A free WordPress promotional website.

Custom Domains

Overall, I always prefer writers to use a custom website and domain name, but I respect this can be intimidating for those new to web design. My example test website previously created at thisbookwasselfpublished.wordpress.com is amateur. It can be found on Google and seen by anyone in the world, but the long domain could be problematic. If desired, you could create a custom domain within WordPress, such as self-published.com. This can be easier to give to people, but it comes with a cost. You are required to purchase a paid plan, which starts at $48 annually, plus the cost of domain registration, which is currently an additional $22 annually. At $70 per year, I believe you would be better served by purchasing an unlimited plan at a traditional web host. I never encourage anyone to pay for blog service through WordPress. They are great for a free blog to better understand the technology surrounding a blog, but the paid plans are expensive for the mediocre service. If you decide to create your own custom domain and blog, I highly encourage you to consider the do-it-yourself approach. Consider the following options.

Self-hosted: I host my website through Namecheap. They rent me a portion of a shared Linux server for less than $50 annually. I can host numerous websites and domain names, configure custom email addresses, and have complete control of my content. This includes the responsibility of site creation, domain forwarding, blog database configuration, and many other technical tasks. If you understand these technologies, nothing beats hosting your own content. If you do not understand the difference between HTML and HTTPS, you should avoid this strategy.

Drag & drop solutions: The easiest option to create a professional website at your own custom domain, such as michaelbazzell.com, is to use a service designed for drag & drop creation. You choose a template, provide your content, and drag anything you see into any place you desire. If you do not have experience building websites and you find WordPress frustrating to control (I do), these options are for you. The most popular service is probably Squarespace, but it is also the most expensive of the three in which I have experience. An annual plan with a custom domain currently costs $144 at Squarespace (squarespace.com), $96 at Strikingly (strikingly.com), or $72 at Weebly (weebly.com). After seeing these prices, you might consider the self-hosted option at Namecheap for $34 annually.

If you expect to self-publish a successful book, and I am confident you will, you really need a professional website at a custom domain related to your work. Many people will judge your website similar to how they would judge the cover of your book. Providing a custom email address to potential and current readers, such as michael@mybook.com (not my address) appears much more professional than Michael12997@gmail.com (also not my email address). Owning your own domain name allows you to move your website and email to any provider desired. This is similar to the benefits of owning your own ISBN as previously explained. Take your online presence very seriously, the world is watching.

Book Purchase Pages

I believe every self-published book should have a complete purchase option page. This should include links to every format of your book, including international print options and all E-book providers. It should be a landing page which can be promoted across various outlets, which allows someone to immediately find the most appropriate purchase option for their area. Figure 9.05 displays mine as an example. This is the page which I reference on my podcast and within my Twitter posts.

The top left portion provides a condensed summary of the book content and a cover image. These are the first details which a potential customer will see. Directly below is a brief summary of each chapter. It includes just enough detail to spark interest within the topics presented. I believe this is vital in order to assure the viewer that there is no fluff in the book. I want to convey that the material is dense and beneficial. I also include an updates section for each of my books. When things change, and any content becomes inaccurate, I can provide updates for readers. This has been very popular with my books about privacy techniques and online investigation methods.

The right column contains numerous purchase links. I typically begin with the print version which includes Amazon affiliate links within the United States and Canada, followed by international links from every Amazon domain. These options typically populate three to fifteen days after publication through KDP. I search my title on amazon.ca, amazon.co.uk, amazon.de, amazon.fr, amazon.it, amazon.es, amazon.co.jp, amazon.com.mx, amazon.com.au, and amazon.in. When the title is available, I add each link, which appears similar to the following. The unique product code should be the same across all countries.

https://www.amazon.ca/dp/B0898YGR58
https://www.amazon.co.uk/dp/B0898YGR58
www.amazon.de/dp/B0898YGR58

When my book gets populated on retail sites such as Walmart and Barnes & Noble, I add those too. This usually occurs about two weeks after publication through IngramSpark. I simply search my title on walmart.com, target.com, and barnesandnoble.com, and then add the purchase links to my website. Sales through these outlets will likely be minimal, but you may see a few impulse purchases of your titles by people already shopping on those sites.

I then offer direct E-book purchase options through Kindle, Apple, Nook, and Kobo. Within three weeks after original publication, you should have active links for your title through every online avenue. Providing your customers an easy way to obtain your title will always translate to more sales. My current page is at https://inteltechniques.com/book8.html.

INTELTECHNIQUES

OSINT TRAINING
PRIVACY CONSULTING
DIGITAL SECURITY

| Online Training | Live Events | Online Resources | Blog | Podcast | Books | Contact |

This Book Was Self-Published: A Technical Guide

There is no shortage of books about becoming a self-published author. Most titles try to motivate you to write your novel, focus on marketing strategies, and explore the occasional self-made millionaire success story. This is not that type of book. This is a technical manual. It includes all of the details the author wishes he would have known before starting his self-publishing journey throughout fifteen books. The technical formalities of creating your own book are missing from the other titles in this space, and likely the reason many people never see their work make it to publication. This book removes the mysteries surrounding hardware configuration, software requirements, document formatting, book content, print publishing, E-book publishing, audiobook publishing, podcast publishing, book piracy, marketing, promotion, affiliate programs, income monitoring, tax reporting, and every other consideration important for your own publication process. This book lays out all of the author's experiences and how he chooses from the platforms available for distribution. Simply stated, this book is about this book. It provides a unique experience which allows you to make it through the nuances of self-publishing.

Print Editions

Amazon-United States
Amazon-Canada
Amazon-UK
Amazon-Germany
Amazon-France
Amazon-Italy
Amazon-Spain
Amazon-Japan
Amazon-Mexico
Amazon-Australia
Amazon-India

Barnes & Noble
Walmart.com
Target.com

E-Book Editions

Amazon
Apple
Nook
Kobo

Bulk Orders

We offer discounted bulk orders with a minimum purchase of 50 copies. Contact us for more details.

Content

CHAPTER 01: Preparation: This chapter walks the reader through the software and hardware configurations required to begin their self-publication journey

CHAPTER 02: Print Formatting: This chapter explains the process of preparing your interior content layout document, including tutorials for trim sizes, spacing, fonts, headers, footers, and all other formalities.

CHAPTER 03: Book Content: This chapter helps with all of the decisions about your content including writing, edits, reviews, and important considerations about your final PDF export.

CHAPTER 04: Covers: Your book will be judged by its cover. This chapter tackles cover design and proper press-ready export.

CHAPTER 05: Print Publishing: This may be the most important chapter of the book. Your self-published submission strategies determine the global availability and royalties. Let's execute perfectly.

CHAPTER 06: E-book Publishing: Publishing an E-book requires more effort than simply uploading your final document. This chapter explains all of the nuances often ignored in order to create a better E-book.

CHAPTER 07: Audiobook Publishing: Audiobook listners are growing. This chapter simplifies the entire audiobook creation process, which can otherwise be overwhelming.

CHAPTER 08: Book Piracy: People will steal your book. This chapter outlines ways to monitor, prevent, and remove violations of your work.

CHAPTER 09: Marketing, Promotion, & Affiliates: If no one knows about your book, you will not sell any copies. This chapter tackles the marketing side of self-publishing and explains how to embrace affiliates.

CHAPTER 10: Podcast Publishing: One of the best ways to promote your book is through a podcast. This chapter explains the entire process.

CHAPTER 11: Income & Taxes: You should monitor your book income and prepare for tax reporting now. This chapter offers several considerations to make it all easier.

Conclusion: A final note to wrap-up the lessons learned throughout the book.

Figure 9.05: A book sales page with numerous purchase links.

Sometimes, I offer discounted bulk pricing of my books. This sounds like an easy decision, but there are many quirks to facilitating the delivery. Before the complete transition from CreateSpace to KDP, bulk sales were easy and reliable. Today, purchasing large orders through KDP can be a gamble. Let's walk through the order process for KDP.

On my sales page, you may have noticed that I offered a bulk purchase option. I typically offer a 20% discount if someone orders ten or more copies directly through me. I accept the order, generate a payable invoice through services such as Square or PayPal, and wait for payment. After payment has been made, I order the books as "Author Copies" directly through KDP, as explained previously, with my author discount. I provide Amazon the address of the purchaser, pay for the books, and then I am hands off. KDP prints the books, Amazon ships them, and you have no hassles. Well, until the complaints roll in.

In my experience, orders of author copies from KDP often have issues. The first is the shipping speed. I recently ordered ten copies of *Extreme Privacy* to be sent to an upcoming live event. The books arrived 25 days after the order. It seems that these orders are given extremely low priority and often do not print for weeks.

The next issue is print quality. After releasing *Extreme Privacy*, I conducted a test. On the same date, I ordered one copy through the official retail site without any discount. I then ordered one author copy through my KDP portal at the discounted rate. The retail copy arrived in two days and looked great. The back page of the book confirmed it was printed at the Lexington, Kentucky printer. The author copy arrived two weeks later and was printed at the San Bernardino, California printer. The author copy looked awful. The interior pages appeared light with faded ink and the cover was not cropped appropriately. The text was off-centered and tilted.

I never base my expectations due to a single order. Unfortunately, I have experienced numerous author copies which were not fit for sale. In one scenario, I ordered 100 books before a live training event and over 20 of them were damaged or improperly cut. I have also had large orders which were perfect. I encourage you to weigh your sales profits versus potential for returns. Fortunately, KDP will accept returns of damaged or poor quality items, but this is a hassle, especially if your customer must do the work.

Bulk sales can be very financially rewarding. If your book has a retail price of $19.99, and your author copies cost $4.50 to print, a 75% royalty awaits you after shipping costs. If you discount the book by 20%, your income drops. Is that extra 10% payment worth the risk? Only you can decide. If you are selling hundreds of books during bulk sales, I believe an argument could be made to go for it. If someone wants to buy 5-10 copies, I can't justify the effort. If you hope to have author copies sent to a book signing event, you must make sure the books arrive ahead of time and someone will be held responsible for them. Always place orders far in advance.

Social Networks

Promotion of your book within your social network profiles can have a large impact on sales. Your Twitter, Facebook, or Instagram profiles will likely be seen by many more people than your website or blog. I encourage you to take advantage of this marketing, but don't go overboard. Blasting ads for your book on your Twitter feed can quickly lead to people unfollowing you. While I do not use Facebook and Instagram, I do have a Twitter account at https://twitter.com/IntelTechniques. I do not claim to be an expert in social network promotions. In fact, I am possibly the worst resource to offer guidance in this area due to my own privacy habits. I can only offer the following considerations.

- **Create free promotional content:** Offer a few nuggets of information from your book within blog posts on your website. Link to these free resources from your social networks and encourage others to promote these posts.

- **Launch a contest:** You could give away a few copies of your newly-published book by inviting social network followers to share why they want the book. Possibly ask them to tag a friend who would also like it. Publicly announce the recipients and encourage them to provide feedback on your profile. This often works well because it makes people aware of your book while also bringing new potential readers towards your profile.

- **Offer a free chapter:** In non-fiction writing, free chapters offer insights into the overall content of the book. If you decide to give away a free chapter of your book, possibly in PDF format, spread the word across your social media profiles. Encourage potential readers to become email subscribers at your website in order to receive the free chapter. This helps build a subscriber list which can increase readers of your blog posts.

- **Consider smaller online communities:** There is much more to the internet aside from Twitter, Instagram, and Facebook. Identifying and posting to a section of Reddit (reddit.com) related to your work could quickly generate new interest in your work.

- **Focus on reading-related communities:** Sites such as Scribophile (scribophile.com) and Goodreads (goodreads.com) allow writers to come together and give each other feedback on their work. Joining these will help you become a better writer and engage with potential customers. You can connect with your audience to answer their questions about your work and participate in online forums where writers and readers discuss books.

Be creative and authentic. If you establish a true connection with your audience, they will follow you wherever you go. In the worst-case scenario, you can turn to your audience and ask them how you can improve. You might be surprised by the honest and raw answers.

Discount Promotional Strategy

Once your E-book is live on Amazon, you might consider a discount price to generate sales activity which may bring in reviews and create more visibility within Amazon. It is easy for your book to get lost in the sea of new releases. You might need to cheat a bit in order to boost your Amazon ranking and assure potential readers that you have a good product. The idea is to lower the price of your E-book to $0.99 for a limited time. This allows people within your circles to purchase your E-book without spending much money. It offers them an opportunity to support your endeavors at little cost. You can then request they leave a review. I have purchased many of my friends' books during this type of promotion, many of which I regrettably have never read. Let's dive into the details of this strategy.

- Within KDP, click the three dots next to your book and select "Edit ebook pricing".

- Change your royalty rate to 35% (required for pricing under $2.99).

- Change your price to $0.99 and re-publish your E-book.

You can now spread the word through personal contacts, your website, and social networks about the promotion. You will not make much in royalties, but the influx of sales could be beneficial. Encourage your audience to review the book if a purchase was made. Since the reviews come from verified purchases, they are likely to be published and impact your overall rating on Amazon. You can reverse the price change whenever you wish. If your book is enrolled in KDP Select, you can start a "Free Book Promotion" or a "Kindle Countdown Deal" to discount your E-book on Amazon. The following will execute this strategy.

- Navigate to your title within your KDP portal.

- Click the "Promote and Advertise" button.

- Choose either the "Free Book Promotion" or a "Kindle Countdown Deal".

You can select up to five days to offer your book for free during each three-month "Select Enrollment" period. You can use all five days at once, one day at a time, or several days at a time. The discounts will automatically start after midnight PST and end exactly at midnight on your final chosen day. You can also end them manually any time you desire. Note that this free strategy only works if you are enrolled in KDP Select, which eliminates the ability to publish your E-book through IngramSpark. I did not choose this enrollment.

Online Reviews

An Amazon book page without any reviews can be a red flag to a potential buyer. However, a new book cannot have any legitimate reviews until purchases have been made. This can create a chicken-and-the-egg situation. I encourage you to politely ask for reviews within the same promotional channels which you announce your book. There is no shame in asking for help. When someone declares on your social network profile that a book was purchased, this is the perfect time to request they leave an honest review on Amazon.

Be warned that reviews are not always positive! I have received my share of negative reviews, and these can be great learning experiences. Some people will leave bad reviews regarding things you cannot control. I received the following negative reviews within the past two months about the print quality from KDP.

"don't know why, but the print on certain pages is unreadable and spotty like they ran out of ink. I don't know how many pages yet, but it's disappointing considering I paid 40.00$+ for the book."

"This might be an awesome book but the printing is the WORST i ever seen in a printed material. And there is not a digital edition available."

While potential readers might ignore these types of reviews since they are not about the content, your overall star score will still be negatively impacted. It is almost impossible to force Amazon to remove a review, unless it contains violent threats. This is part of the game, be prepared now. Accept that you will not make everyone happy, and there are some people incapable of saying nice things. Don't let negative reviews bring you down.

You may feel tempted to leave your own review of your work under an alias. Please do not consider this. First, it is unethical. Second, it violates Amazon's policies. You will likely get caught, Amazon will not post the review, and you could jeopardize your KDP account. The reward is never worth the risk.

Finally, never consider purchasing reviews. At the time of this writing, I could purchase 100 positive Amazon reviews for $750. The provider promises the reviews will be accepted and maintained on the Amazon product profile page. These are scams. Amazon will eventually detect the activity and remove the reviews due to policy violation. At worst, they may remove your book. Even if Amazon allowed the reviews on your page, they are all unverified and somewhat meaningless. Verified reviews from people who actually purchased your book will always receive listing priority and overall contribution to your star score.

Give your book time. Eventually, the reviews will populate on their own through legitimate channels. Don't try to interfere with the process.

Newspaper, Television, and Online Press

Newspapers love to promote local authors. Contacting your local newspaper's lifestyle or entertainment department will usually result in some type of feature, especially if it is a smaller publication. A quick interview, promotional copy, and high-resolution digital cover can lead to a printed and online article about your book. If you have a news station which offers "local spotlight" types of coverage, you may find yourself on television discussing your work. Choose a level of publicity appropriate for your personality. Written articles in a local paper are fairly safe, while an awkward interview on television could be troublesome.

Calling the local news station or sending an unsolicited email to the newspaper is not likely to receive much attention. You need an official book press release. While I am not seeking press coverage of this book, I would create and submit the following press release if I were.

FOR IMMEDIATE RELEASE

THIS BOOK WAS SELF-PUBLISHED
A Technical Guide

September 1, 2020, Los Angeles, CA: Author Michael Bazzell has released his next book, titled This Book Was Self-Published. It serves as a complete technical guide for those interested in stepping into the self-publishing world. It includes all of the details the author wishes he would have known before starting his self-publishing journey throughout eighteen books.

This book lays out all of the author's experiences and how he chooses from the platforms available for distribution. The entire book was written while executing the steps which are discussed. While documenting the formatting of each chapter, the book itself is altered in real-time. All experiences are documented chronologically. Readers experience frustrations and failures together with the author. Simply stated, this book is about this book. It provides a unique experience which allows anyone to make it through the nuances of self-publishing.

The book is currently available through Amazon, Barnes & Noble, and local outlets in both paperback and digital versions. Full resolution book cover and complete description can be downloaded from inteltechniques.com/book8.html.

Michael is available for telephone, video, and in-person interviews beginning September 2, 2020.

Contact:
Michael Bazzell / www.inteltechniques.com / michael@myemail.com

Amazon Associates

The Amazon Affiliate program, officially titled Amazon Associates, is a free affiliate marketing program. It allows you to advertise products from Amazon on your site or blog by creating links to products. When customers click your links and buy products from Amazon, you earn referral fees in the form of a percentage of the sale of whatever they purchase over the next 24 hours. This can generate substantial income. If you provide a link to your book on your site, and a person orders your book from this link, you receive a small kickback from Amazon. However, if that customer also orders $5,000 worth of computer products from Amazon during this purchase, you receive a chunk of the entire order. Let's dive into the details.

The affiliate payments vary for different products and services. I will outline only the most applicable, which were accurate as of July 2020. Amazon can change their rates at any time.

General Merchandise: 4.00%
Physical Books: 4.50%
Music and Videos: 5.00%
Computers & Peripherals: 2.50%
Televisions: 2.00%
Grocery & Health: 1.00%

Amazon also offers one-time "Bounties" which pay a set fee every time a customer uses your link and purchases a specific Amazon service. The following includes the most applicable products.

Amazon Prime Free Trial: $3.00
Audible Audiobook: $0.50
Kindle Unlimited Free Trial: $3.00
Kindle Unlimited Annual Paid Plan: $10.00

Let's put together an example. Assume you have a link on your blog to your book, which sells for $15.00 on Amazon. While shopping, this customer purchases food products valued at $30.00, a clothing item priced at $14.00, and signs up for a free Amazon Prime trial.

Book: $15.00 x 4.50% = $0.68
Food: $30.00 x 1.00% = $0.30
Items: $14.00 x 4.00% = $0.56
Prime: $3.00
Total: $4.54

This order, which was facilitated, fulfilled, and documented by Amazon without any effort on your part, would generate $4.54 to you via a monthly payment. When more customers click your link, you keep adding funds which will be paid to you during your next affiliate deposit. I know a few people who earn over $100,000 annually from Amazon Associates, but they also have a very large audience. Even if you only generate a few extra bucks a month, I believe this program should be activated. Let's walk through the registration process.

- **Create a website or blog:** You must have an active website, blog, app, or YouTube channel to participate in this program. You should also display relative content in order to appear active and authentic to Amazon.

- **Visit the Amazon Associates homepage:** While logged in to your Amazon account, navigate to the Associates page at https://affiliate-program.amazon.com.

- **Create your account:** Click "Sign Up" and follow the prompts to log in to your existing Amazon account. Begin building your Amazon Associates profile by clicking "New Customer". Enter your account information, name, address, and phone number. This can all be the same details already available in your Amazon account.

- **Enter your website address:** Provide any website, blog, or social network addresses which could host an affiliate link.

- **Enter your preferred store ID:** This is usually the same as your primary website or blog name. Provide details about your site and select Amazon topics your links will likely target. When prompted, explain how you drive traffic to your site, such as by checking the "Blogs" option.

- **Confirm contact details:** You may be asked to enter your phone number and allow an automated confirmation call to be placed to you. You will be asked to confirm a four-digit code from the call. Once that is complete, your account should be approved.

- **Enter financial details:** To be paid from Amazon, you must disclose required tax reporting details. These can be identical to the details provided during the self-publishing process. Amazon will deposit your affiliate payments at the same time as KDP deposits, and can be set to the same account. While you can choose an Amazon gift card for payment, income is still reported to the IRS. I encourage you to consider a direct deposit.

You should now have an active Amazon Associates account ready to generate revenue. You should also see the "SiteStripe" bar at the top of any Amazon page while you are logged in to your account. Now, you need to create some affiliate links. My preferred method is the following.

- Navigate to any product, such as your book on Amazon.

- Click the "Text" link within SiteStripe.

- Copy the link created, such as https://amzn.to/3g0A5E1, as seen in Figure 9.06.

- Paste this link on your site, blog, or social network profile.

- Include details about the linked product, such as your book.

When people click your link, they will be forwarded to your book's Amazon page. This special address tells Amazon that the customer was referred by you and places a "cookie" on their computer. This small file will notify Amazon over the next 24 hours that this customer is from you, and Amazon will monitor purchases in order to facilitate an affiliate payment.

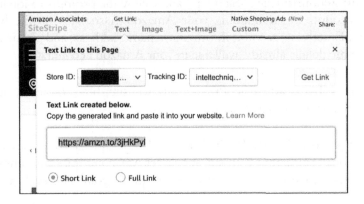

Figure 9.06 The Amazon Associates SiteStripe link generator.

You can monitor activity within your Associates account from the "Earnings" option within the SiteStripe menu bar. This will take you to a daily summary page, which can be easily changed to a monthly view directly under the "Reports" section. The remaining sections of this page display the following items.

- **Clicks:** The total number of clicks on your Amazon Associates links.

- **Ordered Items:** The total number of items ordered through your Associates links.

- **Shipped Items:** The total number of items which were actually shipped to customers.

- **Returned Items:** The total number of returned items.

- **Conversion:** The number of items ordered divided by the number of clicks on your links.

- **Shipped Items Revenue:** The amount of money charged by Amazon for the items.

- **Bonus:** The total revenue earned from Amazon shopping events (not "Bounties").

- **Total Earnings:** Total earnings from referral fees for the selected dates.

- **Items Summary:** A detailed summary of the items ordered as a result of an affiliate link.

The "Payment History" option within the Associates portal displays your previous and upcoming affiliate payments. Similar to book sales, Amazon pays after a delay. As an example, affiliates fees earned during March will be paid at the end of May. Amazon will issue a 1099-MISC form by January 29 of the following year to any Amazon Associates who received payments of $600 or more during the previous year. This will be reported on the same tax form as your royalties.

Amazon has many rules in regard to their affiliates program. I can tell you from experience that they take these rules very seriously and actively monitor for violations. At the beginning of my affiliate usage, my account was suspended for including an affiliate link within an iframe on the home page of my website without referencing a specific item. More recently, I was issued a stern warning for including a link within an email newsletter. Noncompliance with their rules may result in being permanently banned from the program. The following is a summary of their guidelines.

- You must disclose on your site or in your communication that you may be eligible to earn revenue from your recommendations and links. This can be as simple as "some of these are affiliate links", as I have on my website at https://inteltechniques.com/links.html.

- You must not make false or deceptive claims in your recommendations.

- Avoid referring to prices (with some exceptions) since prices frequently change.

- Do not use Amazon affiliate links in offline promotions, E-books, or email.

- Do not use link shorteners on affiliate links. Amazon already shortens links for you.

- You must make at least one sale within 180 days, or your account will be closed. However, you can reapply for the Amazon Associates program after you have made adjustments to your site.

It can take some time to build an audience which will seek links to products from you. I have found success by offering a niche service. Privacy-themed products mentioned within my books and gift ideas on my website have generated some revenue. Book recommendations on my podcast with affiliate links within my show notes bring in new activity. Consider your potential audience and create a valuable online service or blog catered to their needs.

Public Contact Details

Your readers may want to email you, and I believe you should let them. I receive emails from readers daily, many of which have been extremely helpful. Some readers notify me of technical changes which have made portions of my books no longer accurate. I collect all of this information in my notes application and place it at the top of my priorities for the next edition of that title. By the time you read this, I have likely already received email messages about slight changes within KDP or IngramSpark. I highly value this correspondence.

If you are protective of your personal email address, as I am, you can create a special address specifically to put in your books. I previously presented error@inteltechniques.com as a way to contact me directly. This account forwards to a specific folder within my email for weekly viewing. It does not alert me on my phone or present notifications on any device. It is a passive account which I monitor as time permits.

The idea that a reader would take the time to write to me is a boost of confidence. It motivates me to keep publishing. If you begin receiving email from readers regularly, then you are doing something right. Cherish the communication. If you can, you should respond to these emails. However, know your limitations. For many years, I responded to any reader who sent a message. Today, I can't keep up. While relationships with your readers are important, email can be a productivity sinkhole. Every minute you spend on email is a minute you prevent creativity toward your next project. Your readers likely understand that and probably will not expect a response. However, I always respond when someone lets me know of a previously unknown problem with something in a book.

If you begin receiving large amounts of email from readers, expect some criticism. I embrace anything constructive about my work. I have learned a lot from the opposing views of my readers. I have corrected my work in later editions and acknowledged the sources of these changes. However, you will also receive communication which is rude, negative, and occasionally nasty. Disregard it and understand it comes with the territory. Some people insist on telling you that you are wrong, ignorant, or worse. That is OK. **If you are writing something which pleases everyone, and no one disagrees with your content, your words are probably not that interesting.**

This also carries over to social networks. If you have a Twitter account, decide if you want to allow people to send you direct messages. I disabled the feature after a few years when the pending requests became unmanageable. People can still direct public Twitter posts your way, but they will not be expecting a response to a direct message sitting in your inbox.

Newsletters

I highly recommend that you start an email newsletter. This strategy has been a consistent sales avenue for me over the past decade. Announcing a new book to my readers via email typically results in a large sales spike over a three day period. There are countless providers, but I will focus only on MailChimp (mailchimp.com). This service provides free newsletters as long as your recipient list is under 2000 email addresses. After that, a paid plan is required. If you find your list growing past this free tier, I encourage you to shop around, as MailChimp is typically on the expensive side.

Some marketing experts will encourage you to purchase email lists based on the interests of those people and the topic of your book. This is an awful idea. The unsolicited messages will cause people to report you, which will eventually lead to a suspension of your newsletter account. Furthermore, the recipients are highly unlikely to purchase anything. This is simply a waste of time.

I also never recommend adding your entire personal contact list, or the addresses of people who have emailed you about your book, to your newsletter list. This can be considered rude and will likely result in numerous unsubscribe requests. This is another way in which your account may be suspended.

The best formula is to offer readers an option to subscribe to your list, and then give it time. A clean list of newsletter recipients is pure gold. You should place a signup button on your website or blog and encourage your social network followers to join. MailChimp offers an embedded utility which can be placed on practically any website. Users click the button, enter their email, and confirm the subscription. This happens without the need for you to update any records. When you create a newsletter through MailChimp, it automatically goes to anyone active on your list.

By default, MailChimp notifies you every time someone unsubscribes from your newsletter. I encourage you to disable this feature. Otherwise, you might dwell over the reasons that a close friend has withdrawn from your endeavor. I know that I was overly concerned every time someone blatantly declared that they no longer wished to hear from me. This can steal vital time from your next project. It simply doesn't matter, and you have nothing to gain by being alerted every time someone leaves your notification list.

You should start broadcasting regular email newsletters to the people who join your list. Never collect the contacts and wait months to send anything. Don't let your list go stale. You want your readers to be accustomed to hearing from you and receiving beneficial content.

Promotional Review Copies

I have given away hundreds of free copies of my books. While some of these were given out to those who genuinely needed the information quickly, all free copies have some promotional value. Promotional review copies usually fit into one of the following categories.

- **Press review:** Attempts to obtain a review within magazines, newspapers, or other print publications.

- **Online review:** Attempts to obtain a review within a specific website.

- **Organization review:** Attempts to obtain approval to promote a book as an educational aid within a specific organization's website.

- **Contests:** Attempts to obtain promotion at an event due to giveaways of books.

Many book marketing tutorials will tell you to never give away print versions of your books. I disagree with this harsh stance. If you are at the office reading my book on your Kindle, no one knows what you are reading. If you have a print version in your hands, everyone can see you are reading my book. The cover alone can be a great advertisement if a respected colleague is reading a new book. E-books don't make good giveaways. Delivery can be an issue and people don't respect the value of the product. A physical book demands more respect.

I never send an unsolicited or unexpected book for review. That can be a waste of money. Instead, I reach out to the appropriate organizations and ask if they want a free copy. I firmly declare that I have no expectations of a review, but appreciate anything they can share with their audience. The following have been my most successful strategies.

- I sent a free copy of *Extreme Privacy* to a conference associated with network security. I advised the organizers to give it away to an attendee however they preferred. Over 800 people attended the event, and the book was on display the entire day. That night, I saw over 150 new orders outside of the normal scope of sales. My cost was $11.

- I sent two free print copies of an investigative book to an organization related to the world of private investigations. They liked the content and added it to their recommended reading list on their website. They included an Amazon affiliates link to generate their own revenue. This inclusion consistently brings in multiple sales every day. My cost was under $25 for the books. I receive more than that in royalties every day from purchases through their site.

Marketing, Promotion, & Affiliates Checklist

- Create promotional book images.

- Create a free blog.

- Obtain a custom domain.

- Consider self-hosted and drag & drop complete websites.

- Promote your book on social networks.

- Consider a discount promotion.

- Encourage online reviews appropriately.

- Generate newspaper, television, and online press.

- Create an Amazon Associates account.

- Generate and distribute affiliate purchase links.

- Provide public contact information, if desired.

- Create an email newsletter.

- Consider promotional review copies.

CHAPTER TEN
PODCAST PUBLISHING

I started my own podcast in 2016. It was designed to be an outlet for announcing updates to a book which I had released a few months prior to creating the show. It is now my most successful marketing strategy for new releases. The weekly show is an audible business card for any new projects seeking potential customers. Announcing a new book release on the podcast generates more sales than communications through Twitter, newsletters, or my own blog combined. It has never been easier to launch your own podcast, but there are still many nuances which create confusion and a mediocre product. This chapter explains every step I took to create my own show and the maintenance required to keep it going. I warn you that much of this chapter is very similar to the techniques presented while discussing the audiobook process. I feel that the potential for repetitive content is justified as there are many slight variations between the two scenarios. Before we jump into the technicalities, we should understand the power and benefits of hosting a podcast.

Build a connection with your audience: Printed text within a book does not always convey an author's voice and personality. There is something special about hearing someone's voice as they deliver their passion. You may feel personally connected to them as they interview others and share more of their story.

Podcasts are one of the easiest ways to consume content: Non-fiction books can be dry. Listening to an author audibly explain the same content can offer a new perspective. It is difficult (and unsafe) to read while driving, but your audience can devour podcasts during a commute. Some studies claim that 85% of podcast listeners listen to all (or most of) a podcast. That means that once someone starts one of your podcasts, they are more likely to finish the entire episode. People are much less likely to read every word of your emails, newsletters, or social media posts.

Podcasts can make you an authority in your space: The more people who listen to your show and trust your words, the more you become an authority in your industry. The more you are viewed as an influencer and thought leader, the more opportunities may come your way. This can lead to more opportunity, exposure, and sales.

Starting a podcast can be intimidating. Some may be concerned about failing to find listeners or cringing at the sound of their own voice. I can relate to both. However, there is no risk. If no one listens, then no one can be offended or dislike your content. Putting yourself out there is scary, especially with the permanent nature of the internet. However, your show could be the first step toward building a strong brand and engaged audience. Think about your podcast as a way to serve your community instead of making it a perfect representation of yourself.

No more excuses or stalling. Let's begin your podcasting journey.

Plan Your Show

Planning your podcast might be as difficult as recording it. Every podcast is unique, and there is no perfect game plan for them all. I offer the following considerations.

- **Topic:** If your goal is to promote your writing, your podcast should embrace the general topics of your writing. My own podcast serves as a supplement to my two most popular books, so the overall content was obvious for me. You should only consider topics for which you possess a genuine interest. Otherwise, it can feel like an undesired job very quickly. Creating a monthly show about something you do not enjoy can be miserable.

- **Co-hosts:** It can be much easier to start a podcast if you have a co-host. You will usually generate a more engaging conversation if you both share your points of view on a topic, and it can be helpful to have someone to keep things on track. Sharing the responsibilities of editing, promoting, hosting, and costs can also be beneficial. However, there can also be downsides. You should make sure both of you are committed to it for the desired term of the show, or you may experience unfulfilled episodes. Conflicting opinions of the show's structure can be devastating to a new show, so you should make sure you are compatible with the other person. My former co-host left the show in 2018, which left an obvious void in the podcast, but I successfully continued as a solo project.

- **Name:** I find it difficult to create a catchy podcast name. That is probably why mine is so explanatory (The Privacy, Security, & OSINT Show). I encourage you to title your show similar to your book. There should be a marrying of the two if you plan to allow the podcast to accompany the book and generate sales of your title.

- **Style:** Consider the format of the show. Will it be just you? Will you have interviews? Will it be scripted? Will it be dramatic? There is no need to force anything specific, but understand your intended final product. I immediately adopted an "AM radio talk show" style which is easy to record and edit.

- **Length:** I typically like to stay under an hour, but I also serve a very niche audience. I do not believe you should restrict or limit your shows to a specific time, but you should maintain some consistency. Once you build a large audience, your members may unsubscribe if your shows become too short, too long, or too often.

- **Music:** Do you want a theme song? I have gone through two of them and finally have something I like. I believe a consistent piece of short music creates familiarity with the audience. Royalty-free music can be found at https://pixabay.com/music.

Design Your Artwork

Every good podcast needs good artwork. Your show's art is the first impression most people will see as they browse through their favorite podcast app. It also might be the image someone first sees when you share your show on social media. I am no expert on design, so I went with a very simple logo, as seen in Figure 10.01 (left). While I created this within Photoshop, there are easier options which require no technical or artistic abilities. I have previously used the following service.

- Navigate to DesignEvo (designevo.com/logo-maker).

- Select a template which appears appropriate for your show.

- Enter your show name and modify the font, size, or placement as desired.

- Click the download option, then click the link labeled "Download a low-resolution".

- Create a free account and confirm their terms of service.

If the downloaded logo is too small for your needs (300 x 300 pixels), you could take a screen capture of the design on your screen. Services such as SoundCloud insist on a large logo which they will compress. In my test, the working copy on my screen was 2000 x 2000 pixels. I used my Mac screen capture utility (command-shift-4) and drew a box around the image within the web browser. My research could not find any terms of service which prevented this capture and usage of the file as long as attribution to the service was included anywhere the image is present. If you do not want to provide attribution of your logo, you could play with the service to identify a design idea and replicate within Photoshop. The images seen in Figure 10.01 (middle and right) were both created and downloaded using DesignEvo.

Figure 10.01: Simple logos for podcasts.

Prepare For Episodes

There are many podcasts which seem very unorganized. It may be a group of friends in a basement hoping that if they hit record a show will somehow appear by the end of the night. I try to avoid this pitfall. I never record anything until I know I have the potential for a full show. At any given time, I have a list of approximately ten show topic ideas which need to mature. As I think about ways to tackle a specific show topic, I add notes. Once I see that a full show exists, I move the topic to its own show notes.

I first plot out the show within Standard Notes, which was explained previously. I want a written guide to the entire show available to me. I want to know the order of topics, and I think about the flow from one to the other. This is a delicate balance for me. I want enough detail prepared to adequately cover each topic, but I do not want to plan every word which will be said. I prefer things to flow naturally and I do not script my shows. I believe that preparing a script to be read verbatim often sounds over-rehearsed and flat. I prefer to go for it, which leads to imperfection, but usually provides a more authentic experience.

I am fortunate that I present topics which are of great interest to me. Privacy, Security, and OSINT are my passions, so I feel honored to have an audience that wants to hear my views. I also learn a ton from doing the show. I am forced to research things until I understand every detail, which benefits me more than the audience. If you do not have a deep interest in the topic of your own show, you will get burned out quickly.

Listener feedback can drive show topics. The majority of my own show topics are originally suggested by listeners. Offering an email address for listener feedback can be extremely valuable. It helps you understand what you can do better and where your audience wants the show to go. Sometimes, I create entire shows from listener questions, and these are often the most downloaded episodes. Offering a way for listeners to contact you can also have negative consequences. I receive negative and hateful emails daily. To me, this is simply a sign of a growing audience. I noticed the first uptick of hateful comments after surpassing 20,000 listeners per show. If this happens, ignore it. Internet trolls will always find a way to spread negativity. If they are less than 1% of your listeners, you are doing great!

You may want to focus some of your podcast time on generating income for your show. I open each segment quickly promoting my books and then move on to the content. You could recommend a book and provide an affiliate link or accept sponsors. Typically, podcasters earn around $20 per ad, per 1000 downloads, within 30 days of an episode's release. If you have 5,000 listeners within 30 days of releasing a show, a sponsor might pay you $100 to read an ad or recommend a product. While I have had sponsorships in the past, I completely eliminated them from my show. I wanted to be able to be unbiased with my content without fears of upsetting a sponsor. I also don't enjoy the sales aspect while constantly courting potential sponsors. You may be good at that. I know many people earning thousands of dollars per show.

Record Your Audio

Once you have an outline and any general formalities determined, it is time to record your first show. First consider the following in reference to your vocal capture. Note that much of this chapter was previously presented within the audiobook portion of this book. However, many modifications have been made for podcast recording, as explained throughout this chapter.

- **Microphone:** For amateur or first-time podcasting, I recommend a USB microphone with condenser, specifically the Yeti made by Blue. If you are on a tight budget, I have also used the Snowball made by Blue. The Yeti can be found for $100 while the Snowball is commonly sold for under $50. I never recommend headset earbud-style microphones or embedded mics within devices such as a laptop or mobile device. That will deter listeners from coming back. My Yeti is always in the "Cardiod" setting, which can be controlled by the knob on the back. This mode records sound sources which are directly in front of the microphone.

- **Environment:** I doubt many readers possess an isolated sound booth for perfect vocal capture. If you have a decent microphone, a dedicated small sound-proof area is not vital. I record in my home office with good results. If you want to create a better recording, consider capturing your audio from within a closet. If that is overkill for your needs, draping a hung blanket around your back and sides can have a huge impact.

Now that you have your vocal recording area ready, you need some software which will convert your voice into a digital file. There are countless audio recording software suites which range from minimalistic apps to expensive professional options. If you are already familiar with something common, such as Garage Band, then you should use that. If you have no experience with digital audio recording, I recommend Audacity (audacityteam.org). This free software can be installed on Windows, Mac, or Linux, and provides all of the basic features we need without excess bells and whistles. This doesn't mean that the software is self-explanatory; there will still be a learning curve. However, I will provide some guidance on the basics.

Hardware Detection & Selection: Make sure your microphone is connected and recognized by your operating system before launching Audacity. Open the system settings for Windows or Mac and make sure the input volume is maximized for the microphone. Within Audacity, choose your microphone from the top entries, as seen in Figure 10.02. If supported, choose a stereo recording.

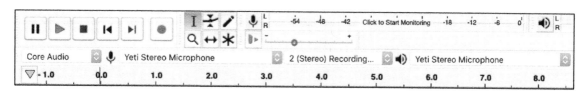

Figure 10.02: The Audacity hardware selection menus.

Track Creation: Within Audacity, we need to add a new track, which will capture your voice. In the Audacity file menu, select "Tracks", "Add New", then "Stereo Track". This will create a new entry within your software, as seen in Figure 10.03.

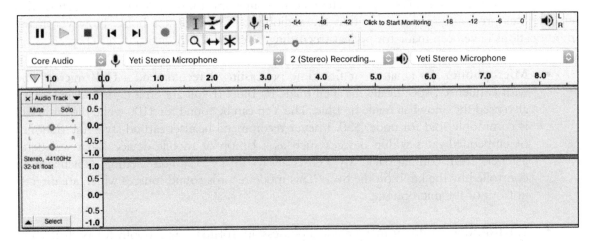

Figure 10.03: The Audacity audio track.

Audio Recording: Click the red circle to begin your recording. Ensure that you see the visual representation of captured audio, as seen in Figure 10.04. The black square will stop the recording. As long as your cursor is placed at the end of any track, the red circle will begin recording at the designated location. If you place the cursor within previously recorded audio, it will record at that chosen place. This can risk losing or overwriting audio, so use caution.

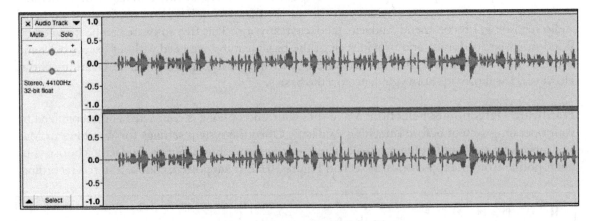

Figure 10.04: A recorded audio track.

Edit Your Audio

You could publish your audio file as it was recorded, but that will likely result in a problematic show. I have never recorded a podcast which required no editing. Anticipate problems now, but know that you can easily modify the audio in order to create a polished product. Consider the following.

Content Removal: When I create a show by myself, with only my vocals, I never stop recording. Even if I need to pause to gather my thoughts, I let the recording go. My Yeti microphone provides a physical mute button which is beneficial for visually identifying portions of my audio without sound. When finished, I can select any silent areas by dragging the cursor throughout them, and click the delete key on the keyboard. When mastered, no one will suspect your podcast was not created perfectly within one take. Figure 10.05 displays a selection of silence for removal. If you need to zoom in to see the file better, use the "View" and "Zoom" menu options.

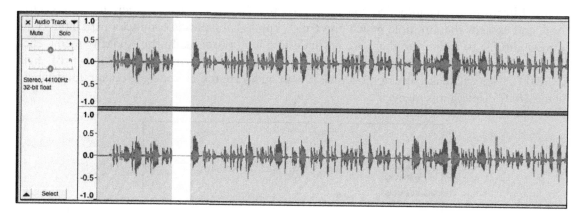

Figure 10.05: Selection of silence within Audacity for removal.

Sound Amplification: Most vocal recordings are "quiet" and may need amplified. I typically need to amplify my recordings by 2.0 decibels. If you need to boost your recording, double click the audio wave within a track to select the entire recording. Then click on "Effect" in the menu and choose "Amplify". Set your desired level, such as 2.0 to 3.0, and click "OK". Figure 10.06 displays my enhanced audio file. While it may appear visually similar to the previous image, the overall volume is higher. I encourage you to play this file while playing a professional podcast in your browser. Which is louder? Depending on your microphone and environment, you may need to boost your audio levels much higher. Once you reach a volume which is close to the professional shows, we can remember this setting for future usage.

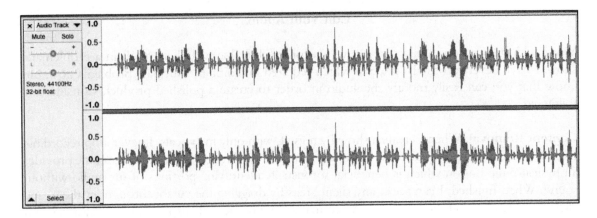

Figure 10.06: An amplified Audacity audio track.

Sound Limiting: If you amplified your track, you may have a few places where the audio is too "hot" and exceeds the threshold which prevents "clipping". I typically conduct a hard limit to the entire audio file to make sure there are no undesired loud portions. In the Audacity menu, click "Effect" then "Limiter". Choose "Hard Limit" in the menu and change the "Limit to (dB)" field to "-2.00". This will make sure no portions of your audio are too close to the maximum decibels. Figure 10.07 displays this menu.

	Limiter	
Type:	Hard Limit	
Input Gain (dB) mono/Left:	0.00	
Input Gain (dB) Right channel:	0.00	
Limit to (dB):	-2.00	
Hold (ms):	10.00	
Apply Make-up Gain:	No	
Manage Preview	? Cancel OK	

Figure 10.07: An Audacity hard limiter dialogue.

Additional Tracks: You can repeat this process for additional tracks if you want to add audio outside of a main vocal recording. This can exceed the scope of this chapter quickly, but I offer the following.

- You can highlight any audio and cut (ctrl-x / cmd-x) and paste (ctrl-v / cmd-v) practically anywhere desired. This can be helpful when you want to splice new audio into a previously recorded section.

- You can create a section of silence on a track if it needs delayed due to audio present on another track. Click on "Generate" in the menu and choose "Silence". Enter the duration desired.

Additional Tips: There are hundreds of options within Audacity which may be beneficial to podcast hosts. I rely heavily on the following.

- **Tone:** Clicking "Generate" and "Tone" presents an option to redact audio. I use this when a guest curses (in order to prevent an "explicit" warning from Apple) or I need to protect the identity of a person on the other end of a phone call (such as an accidental reference to a name). I prefer to use the "Sine" option within this menu, with a frequency of 400 and amplitude of 0.2.

- **Fade:** Any time I present audio in my show, I prefer to fade it out at the end. This sounds better than a hard break. I select the end of the audio by clicking and dragging the cursor, then choose "Effect" and "Fade Out". This can also be used to introduce audio with the "Fade In" option.

- **Sync-Lock Tracks:** If you have multiple tracks due to an interview, you may want to lock them for editing by clicking "Tracks" and then "Sync-Lock Tracks". This allows you to edit all tracks at once. I typically use this to delete undesired silence or an entire section of an interview from all tracks. This prevents everything from becoming out of sync.

An entire book could be written on the intricacies of Audacity or any other audio recording software. I encourage you to spend considerable time playing with audio files if you plan to continue creating podcasts. I learn something new every month.

Recording Interviews: If you plan to have guests on your show, you need to prepare to capture their audio. There are premium services, such as Zencastr (zencastr.com), which simplifies this process, but they possess their own risks. I once participated on a Zencastr recording with a colleague on his own show, and the entire audio was lost forever. Apparently, there was a crash on behalf of Zencastr's servers, and we both wasted a couple of hours. The show was never re-recorded and neither of us has trusted Zencastr since.

I prefer to manage this myself. I currently use Audio Hijack (rogueamoeba.com/audiohijack) on my Mac laptop. It captures audio from any application on my computer and pairs it with my own microphone. I can place a call through a service such as Google Voice and record both sides of the conversation within Audio Hijack. I have used this program during every published interview and telephone call since 2016.

Host Your Audio

There are many ways to host the audio files which deliver your podcast. They range from free temporary storage to permanent paid archiving. I always recommend that everyone begin with an easy free option which can later be converted into a permanent paid solution if desired. I also want the ability to monitor download stats, replace tracks when needed, disable comments, schedule episode releases, and embed a player on any website. Oh, and I want it to be affordable compared to other premium services. Because of these demands, I currently recommend Soundcloud (soundcloud.com) as a podcast host. The following steps will open an account and start the free tier of service.

- Navigate to https://soundcloud.com/ and click "Create Account".

- Provide a valid email address and password when prompted.

- Provide an age and gender if prompted.

- Enter the title of your potential podcast if prompted.

- Click the link in the confirmation email sent by SoundCloud.

- Click the three dots in the upper-right, and select "Settings".

- Click the "Content" tab, and provide the name of your podcast in the "Custom feed title".

- Provide your name in the "Custom author name" section.

- Choose a general topic of your podcast in the "Category" field.

- Enable the "Include in RSS feed" option and click "Save changes".

- Document the "RSS feed" URL for future use.

- If desired, modify the remaining sections as appropriate to your privacy needs.

You now have a SoundCloud account configured to serve as a podcast host and feed. The free tier is limited to a total of three hours of available content. If you reach this limit, you can delete an older episode to make room for something new. If desired, you can shuffle the free content indefinitely as long as you never exceed the limitations. You are now ready to upload your first episode. The following steps should serve as a guide.

- Log in to your SoundCloud account and click the "Upload" option in the top menu.

- Select the audio file of your recording and begin the upload.

- Enter the title, genre, topics (tags), and description of your episode.

- Upload an image of your podcast artwork and click "Save".

Note that the free plans from SoundCloud are missing a few features. "Pro" plans allow you to store unlimited episodes, replace audio files in case of an error, schedule dates and times for an episode's release, disable comments, and disable statistics. I currently possess a Pro account, which can be seen at https://soundcloud.com/user-98066669. My cost is $144 annually, and I have almost 200 weekly shows archived. I encourage you to embrace a free account and test the waters. You may find a recurring show difficult to manage. If you decide to continue past the limitations of the free account, upgrading is recommended and easy.

With SoundCloud, you are never limited to a set number of downloads or episodes. If you do not anticipate over a few hundred listeners, are not sure if you will stick to podcasting after a dozen shows, and want a completely free solution, I recommend Anchor (anchor.fm). Anchor is owned by Spotify and is completely free. You receive unlimited free hosting, bandwidth, and listener analytics.

However, there is a catch. Anchor technically owns your feed and has the right to insert ads if desired. Unless you begin experiencing thousands of weekly downloads, you may not ever have an ad in your show. They also use a custom internal email address when submitting your show to Apple, which makes me nervous. Most of these issues can be eliminated with various workarounds, but you never know what will come next. Overall, it is a great place to test the waters and try out podcasting without any financial risk. If your show takes off, I would move to a paid product which gives you more control of your content.

You can create a new account at https://anchor.fm/signup and upload your show. I am hesitant to offer explicit tutorials in regard to uploading content and modifying the configurations for your show due the constant changes on Anchor's website. With the recent acquisition of Anchor by Spotify, I suspect we will see further changes in the near future, including the elimination of completely free podcast hosting. However, signing up now may lock you into a free account later.

If neither of these options suits your needs, I would research other services such as Libsyn (libsyn.com), Podbean (podbean.com), and Spreaker (spreaker.com). I have had experience with all of the services listed here. Of those, I found SoundCloud to be the easiest option without the bells and whistles which generally raise the fees of other options.

Publish Your Audio

You can share a link to your SoundCloud page to potential listeners, but you are missing the majority of users. Very few people listen to podcasts through a static web page. Instead, they use various applications which fetch shows from a feed. To present your podcast within the search feature of their chosen app, you need to announce your RSS feed to various services. The following should all be considered, in order of priority.

Apple Podcasts: Most people who own an iPhone, iPod, or iPad rely on the default podcasting application available from Apple. Their closed system requires submission of new shows through their own network, which can be quite problematic for those without an Apple device. If you own an iPhone or Mac computer, the following steps will submit your show for review.

- Navigate to https://podcastsconnect.apple.com and sign in with your Apple ID.

- From the "My Podcasts" screen, click the "+" in the upper-left.

- Provide your podcast RSS feed identified previously and click "Validate".

- Confirm your show details and click "Submit".

- Within 48 hours, your show should be available within the Podcasts app and iTunes Store.

This process is fairly painless if you have an Apple ID and device. However, it can be difficult for those without this luxury. If you do not possess Apple hardware, replicate the following in order to launch your own show.

- Navigate to https://appleid.apple.com and select the option to create a new ID.

- When prompted, provide your name, address, telephone number, and other details.

- Navigate to https://podcastsconnect.apple.com and sign in to your Apple ID.

At this point, you will likely be greeted with a notice that you do not qualify to upload content to Apple Podcasts. This is because Apple now requires an Apple ID account which has been associated with an iTunes account or App Store to be used for new podcast submission. Typically, an Apple computer or mobile device is required to meet this demand. I find this to be an unfair practice by Apple, but we have no control over their policies. I offer the following options for your consideration.

- **Windows Alternative:** If you have a Windows computer, you can download iTunes from the Apple website at https://www.apple.com/itunes. At the time of this writing, associating your account with this software satisfied the requirements to upload podcasts. After you install the software, click on "Account" and "Sign In" within the iTunes menu. Enter your previous Apple ID credentials and confirm any dialogue screens. From your own computer, refresh the web page on your Apple Podcasts account, and you should see the option to submit your show.

- **Friend's Computer:** If you know someone with an Apple computer, you can use it to activate your account. Open the App Store, click on "Store" in the menu, and choose the option to "Sign Out". Then sign in with your new Apple ID and confirm that you want to activate an iTunes account. You may be asked for payment sources, but this can be skipped by choosing "None". When finished, sign out of your account and allow your friend to sign back in. From your own computer, refresh the web page on your Apple Podcasts account and you should see the option to submit your show.

- **Public Computer:** Many libraries and hotels offer Apple computers with internet access to customers. Replicate the previous steps and be sure to log out of your account when finished. When you return home, change the password to your Apple ID for extra security.

Stitcher: Many people who do not have Apple devices rely on Stitcher or Spotify to fetch podcasts. Navigate to https://partners.stitcher.com/join and click "Join Us Today". Enter the RSS feed of your podcast and follow the additional prompts. Your show should be added to their environment within 24 hours.

Spotify: Navigate to https://podcasters.spotify.com/ and click "Get Started". Create an account and look for an option labeled "Add or claim podcast". If necessary, navigate directly to the page at https://podcasters.spotify.com/submit and submit your RSS feed address. Your show should be added to their environment within 24 hours.

Google Play Music: Android users may rely on Google for all media content. The Google Play platform is the final mandatory option if you want significant reach. Navigate to https://play.google.com/music/podcasts/publish and log in to your Google account. If you do not have one, create one on this page. After you are logged in, choose the option to submit your podcast. This should also submit your show to Google Podcasts. You can confirm this by going to https://search.google.com/devtools/podcast/preview and searching for your show. It may take up to 72 hours to see results.

iHeart Radio: This service, as well as the options remaining in this section, may already pick up your show from the previous resources. However, you should submit your show through their official process. Navigate to https://www.iheart.com/content/submit-your-podcast and provide your email address, podcast title, and RSS feed. You do not need to create an account. Agree to any terms and click "Submit". You should see your show within their app after 48 hours.

Everything Else: There are hundreds of potential podcast streams which allow submission of a show. Most will pick up your podcast from the previous resources within 30 days, but it never hurts to continue the spread of your project. Please consider the following services.

Pandora: ampplaybook.com/podcasts/   **Radio:** radio.com/podcast-submission
Pod Directory: poddirectory.com/submit   **Deezer:** podcasters.deezer.com
Pod Bean: podbean.com/site/user/login   **Player.fm:** player.fm/suggest?method=post

Promote Your Audio & Monitor Listenership

Ideally, you will have your podcast launched before you publish your book. This way, you can include a note to readers to transition them to your podcast for updates and announcements. I always reference my show in the conclusion section of every book. This brings in more listeners, which brings in more future book sales. It is a complete cycle of promotion. If you use social networks, promoting your show across the basics can be beneficial. Every time I record a new episode, I conduct the following.

- Upload the show to SoundCloud (soundcloud.com/user-98066669).

- Create a blog post with show notes and a link to the episode (inteltechniques.com/blog).

- Post the show to my Podcast archive on my site (inteltechniques.com/podcast.html).

- Post a Tweet about the show with a link to my site (twitter.com/IntelTechniques).

- Confirm the show within Apple Podcasts, Stitcher, Spotify, etc.

SoundCloud, and any other podcast host, should notify you of the overall "Downloads" of each episode. This can serve as a guide to know the growth of your audience, but these numbers are misleading. If a person has subscribed to your feed in a podcasting app, the file gets downloaded automatically. This counts as a download even if the person never plays the file. This can lead to a HIGHER number of listeners than quoted on SoundCloud. On the other side, some services cache their own copy of your show and distribute it to listeners. This can result in hundreds of people listening, but one download documented. This can result in a LOWER number of listeners than quoted. I encourage you to monitor your stats only for growing numbers every month. Don't get caught up in the actual number.

Podcast Publishing Checklist

- Plan your new podcast.

- Design your show artwork.

- Record your audio.

- Amplify your sound files.

- Limit the peak sound of your audio files.

- Create an account at SoundCloud.

- Host your podcast with an RSS feed.

- Distribute your feed to all popular podcasting services.

- Promote your show.

- Monitor listener downloads.

CHAPTER ELEVEN
INCOME & TAXES

Hopefully, your book is selling well and you have the privilege of dealing with payments from your chosen publisher(s). This also brings the responsibility of dealing with taxes. I encourage all writers to monitor sales through any channels selected during the publishing process. This chapter will help you understand the various reporting platforms and offer some considerations toward taxation of your income.

Legal Warning: I am not an attorney or accountant. I offer no legal advice regarding income or taxes. Consult with an attorney or accountant before executing any strategies mentioned in this chapter.

Monitoring your online sales has many benefits. First, it helps you prepare for the income you will be receiving (and prepare for the taxes you will be paying). This can work against you as well. If you are expecting Amazon to drop a large deposit into your checking account, while writing checks against this potential deposit, you may find the payments to be less than expected. Be aware of all banking activity and do not allocate money for expenses which may not be present.

More importantly, watching purchase data is quite rewarding. Seeing sales in real time helps justify the numerous hours put into your project. It allows you to take a moment and enjoy the fruits of your labor. This is also quite motivating. At the end of every book I write, I promise myself it will be the last. After a few months, I watch the sales trickle in and start to get the itch to begin a new project. Without the ability to see this data, I may never plot another title.

Publishing through traditional publishers can never replicate the granular detail available to you about your sales. With a big outfit, you would be lucky to receive a quarterly payment with a vague statement about unit sales, advances, and expenses. You will not see real-time orders through Amazon or monthly notices of pending deposits. You would also likely see a 10-15% royalty instead of the 40-60% options seen with my strategies. Self-publishing gives you much more control and transparency.

Finally, you can enjoy the comfort knowing that all royalty payments are going directly to you. A traditional publisher pays the salaries of editors, public relations experts, and sales departments before considering your share. You reap the rewards of your hard work and may experience substantial passive income as your book continuously sells copies daily.

Monitor KDP Sales

At the time of this writing, there were two KDP portals available for sales data, and I will explain each. The standard "Reports" portal available to logged in members immediately displays a sales dashboard announcing overall sales of all titles over the past 30 days. However, this can be misleading. While this displays daily E-book purchases near to real time, print books are only posted after they have shipped, which can be days after an order. Also, this view does not account for returns which may result in decreased royalties. Finally, the "Royalties Earned" near the bottom is not the payment you will receive next month. It is the "live" royalties for the past month which can change without notice. We should have an understanding of how KDP issues payments to self-publishers.

KDP pays royalties every month, approximately 60 days after the end of the month in which the sale was reported. Sales made through Expanded Distribution are paid approximately 90 days after the end of the month in which the sale was reported. KDP issues separate payments for each Amazon marketplace in which you distribute your title. This can seem confusing, so let's break it down with two examples.

- You publish your book on January 1. It sells 100 copies between January 1-31 through Amazon and 25 copies through Expanded Distribution. Your first payment of these royalties will be paid near the end of March and includes all sales made through Amazon. At the end of April, you will be paid the royalties earned through Expanded Distribution.

- The payment you receive at the end of August is for the total royalties earned during the month of June from Amazon, along with any Expanded Distribution royalties earned during the month of May.

The main reason for the delay of payment is returns. If a customer purchases your book, he or she has 30 days to return it to Amazon for a full refund. When this happens, the royalty from that sale is deducted from your potential payment. Once the window of opportunity for refunds is over, Amazon processes a payment at the end of that month. This way, any money cleared for a royalty payment cannot be taken away from you.

The sales dashboard is beneficial to view daily sales trends, but never count on it for final payment. Clicking the "Payments" tab identifies previous and pending royalty payments into your bank account. Fortunately, it is split into regions to identify books sold through international Amazon marketplaces. Note that payments are displayed in various country currencies.

The "Historical" tab is beneficial for viewing sales trends throughout the lifetime of the account. Figure 11.01 displays my book sales since 2012. I am able to instantly see sales spikes during new releases or marketing attempts.

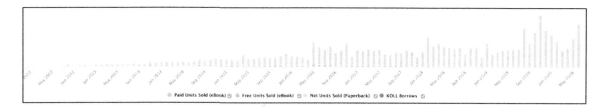

Figure 11.01: The historical KDP sales view.

The new KDP Reports dashboard, which is currently in a "beta" stage, but may be the default view when you read this, can be found at https://kdpreports.amazon.com/dashboard. This view provides more daily granular detail about book sales and focuses more on real-time orders instead of shipped units. I prefer this format. It displays estimated daily sales, royalties, and title summaries. The "View Royalties Estimator" link at the bottom displays current month-to-date orders, but does not allow historical views of past months. The "View Orders" link from the main dashboard allows you to search for order data as far back as 2018. The "Kindle Edition Normalized Pages" (KENP) section identifies overall pages read by members of the Kindle Unlimited program, if you chose to enroll. This is typically a very small payment. Hopefully, KDP will incorporate all other reports previously mentioned before forcing members to switch to this new format.

I encourage you to monitor your daily, weekly, and monthly sales in order to understand the size of your audience. This also helps identify any successful marketing campaigns which may have launched on specific dates which caused a spike in sales. However, don't focus on the overall royalty payments until your book has been selling copies for several months. I have experienced a large amount of sales within the first few weeks and then see that trickle to almost nothing by the third month. Don't assume that strong sales continue forever.

Some readers will return books for a full refund. This may be due to a bad print, dislike of your content, or just rude behavior. I know someone who buys books, reads them quickly, and then returns them even if he enjoyed the content. When Amazon suspends his account, he creates a new one and repeats the routine. If you see returned products in your portal, don't become too consumed with the potential reasons. It may have nothing to do with your writing.

The best way to identify any returns is to generate a report on the "Sales Dashboard" screen near the bottom of your "Reports" portal. This includes a column titled "Units Refunded" which allows you to determine the title, date, royalty, and currency of any returns. You will never see any details about the customer's name, address, email, or any other identifiable information. Some Amazon accounts have the ability to see vague data about the general location of purchases, but this data is unreliable. It once showed me that hundreds of books were sold in Chicago, Illinois. I later learned that this was a shipping stop for all books sold in Canada. If you have enrolled in Amazon's Author Central, you can see this data at https://authorcentral.amazon.com/gp/metrics/geo.

Monitor IngramSpark Sales

After logging in to your IngramSpark account at https://myaccount.ingramspark.com, you should be forwarded to their membership portal. The sales information is more data driven and not as easy to digest. Generating a query which meets the demands of their reporting infrastructure can be a chore. However, we can recreate most of the features available through KDP. This option is only appropriate for those who followed the KDP and IngramSpark combination previously explained. After clicking on the "Reports" menu, you should see the following options with explanations of each service.

- **E-book Sales Report:** You must select the date range, region, currency, and compensation type before a report can be generated. The report reflects sales and not actual royalty payments. Returns will be deducted from current or future payouts. If searching for sales with less than a year's worth of data, results can be displayed on the screen. If searching longer than one year, a report must be sent via email.

- **Print Sales Report:** Similar to the previous option, you must select the date range, region, currency, and compensation type before a report can be generated. The report reflects sales and not actual royalty payments. Returns will be deducted from current or future payouts. If searching for sales with less than a year's worth of data, results can be displayed on the screen. If searching longer than one year, a report must be sent via email.

- **Publisher Compensation Payments Report:** This option generates a report of your royalty payments from IngramSpark. This includes printed books sold outside of Amazon and E-books outside of the Kindle ecosystem. You must enter a valid email address to obtain the report.

- **Publisher Compensation Unpaid Invoices Report:** This option displays upcoming payments of royalties.

- **Transaction History:** This provides a summary report of sales history and any credits applied, including chargebacks and other adjustments.

- **Pre-Order Report:** This option generates a report of orders which have been submitted for a title which has not been released. This is not used in our demonstrations.

Overall, I have always experienced great delays from the time of sales until I see entries within any of these reports. We have basically no way of knowing if the reporting or royalty payments are accurate. I stopped trying to confirm if sales seemed to appropriately match payments. I only use this portal as a notification of approximate sales of my titles outside of Amazon. In my experience, orders through IngramSpark are a small percentage of total sales. Amazon has always been the bulk of purchases for my titles.

Monitor Payments

Verifying payments received is important, especially during the first few months of royalties. While Amazon has always been accurate with my payments, things can go wrong. I recommend comparing all monthly payments to your bank with the "Payments" tab within your KDP portal to make sure they match. Then, take a look at the historical record to make sure the approximate numbers align. As I write this in July of 2020, I conducted the following.

- Identify the upcoming payments due at the end of the month, which reflect sales from May, on the "Payments" tab in the default portal.

- Conduct a custom search for the entire month of May within the "Sales Dashboard" in KDP. The payments at the bottom should match exactly, unless you had returns.

- Confirm the bank deposits match these numbers.

Deposits from Amazon are split into royalty payments from various regions, and any affiliate payments are made the same day as royalties. Figure 11.02 displays a redacted view of my deposits from June of 2020. The first five entries are from Amazon Europe, which include payments from United Kingdom, France, Spain, Italy, and Germany. The sixth entry is from Canada, while the seventh is from Japan. The eighth entry is from Amazon US while the final entry is the affiliates payment. Your order may be different, but can always be confirmed with the previous methods.

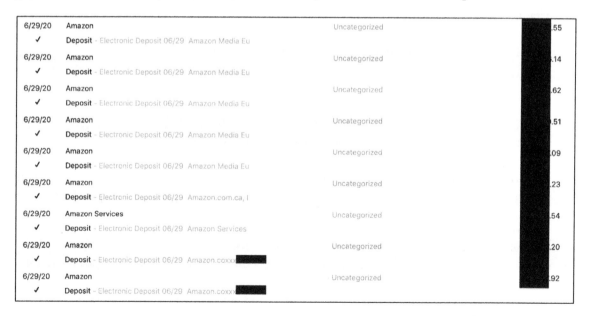

Figure 11.02: A bank statement displaying Amazon deposits.

KDP Tax Reporting

Amazon (KDP) issues a digital IRS Form 1099-MISC on or before January 31 of each year for any accounts of U.S. authors which have been paid a minimum of $10.00 the previous year. In other words, if you sold more than a couple of copies of your book online, the IRS knows this, and you must report the income. Unless you are subject to mandatory withholding of taxes, which is extremely rare, Amazon does not withhold any taxes from your payments. At the time of this writing, KDP tax forms can be accessed online with the following steps.

- Sign in to KDP and click "Your Account" at the top of the page.

- Follow the instructions for two-step verification.

- Under "My Account", click "Tax Information".

- Click "View/Provide Tax Information".

- Scroll down to the "Year-End Tax Forms" section.

- Click "Find Forms" and "Download" next to your desired form.

Figure 11.03 displays a redacted copy of my own 1099-MISC form from 2019. Let's discuss a few important considerations within this document.

- The "Payer's TIN" is Amazon's EIN.

- The "Recipient's TIN" is your IRS reporting number, such as an SSN or business EIN.

- Box "2 Royalties" is the overall money paid to you from Amazon. This number should match the total of all monthly royalty payments in the designated year.

- Box "7 Nonemployee Compensation" is the overall non-royalty payments paid to you from Amazon. This is typically any affiliate fees earned through customer purchases.

The difference between boxes 2 and 7 are drastic. Typically, nonemployee compensation is taxed higher than royalties. The amount in box 7 is likely prone to federal tax, state tax, and self-employment tax (15.3%). However, royalty payments (box 2) are not always prone to self-employment tax. Whether or not your royalty income is subject to self-employment taxes depends on your current profession. If you are active in any profession related to the royalties you receive, the money will likely be considered compensation subject to self-employment taxes. If not, you may not be assessed the self-employment tax. Let's consider two examples.

- An author who wrote a book about gardening, but is not engaged in gardening for profit, would typically not have to pay self-employment taxes on the book's royalties.

- An author who wrote a book about tax-consulting, who happens to be a full-time accountant, would typically need to pay self-employment taxes on the book's royalties.

Amazon (KDP) issues a digital IRS Form 1042-S on or before March 15 of each year for any accounts held by non-U.S. authors which have been paid a minimum of $0.49 the previous year. This form is an informational statement that the IRS requires Amazon to provide. The form is sent to non-U.S. authors who received U.S. sourced income during the previous calendar year. This form should be provided to the tax professional in your own country who will be assisting with tax reporting and payments.

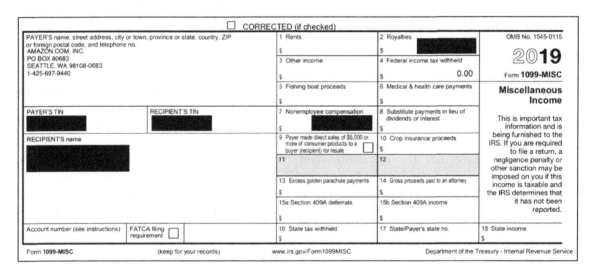

Figure 11.03: A 1099-MISC form issued by Amazon.

There is a lot of confusing area here. Please contact a tax professional in order to determine your own tax responsibilities. Remember that every payment received from any self-publishing service will be reported to the IRS. Be sure to match this reporting on your own tax returns. This also applies to IngramSpark and any other service which has sold your product. Take note of the source of all payments. After January 31 of the year following your payments, track down the digital tax forms offered by each company. Most services will send you an email once the forms are available. IngramSpark recently stopped sending IRS 1099 forms to customers, stating that they were no longer required to do so due to the definition of their service. This does not mean you do not have to pay taxes on those proceeds. Overall, it is up to YOU to report and pay taxes as a self-employed author and not the services which handle your sales. Keep good records and sleep well at night without fears of an IRS audit.

Tax Deductions

If you begin making substantial income from your writing, you will likely claim your 1099-MISC form on a Schedule C with the IRS when you file your income taxes. You should also consider deducting your expenses related to writing and selling your books. The following is a list of potential expenses which may qualify for a full or partial deduction from the taxes due from your royalty income.

Computer(s)

Computer peripherals

Printer(s)

Paper and office supplies

Proof copies of books

Final copies of books

Promotional copies of books

Shipping fees

Website fees

Software and licensing

Advertisement and marketing

Internet access

Home Office Deduction: Your tax professional may recommend a claim for a home office deduction. If you use part of your home for business, such as writing your books, you may be able to deduct expenses for the business use of your home. The home office deduction is available for homeowners and renters and applies to all types of homes. People using the IRS "regular method" must determine the actual expenses of their home office, including mortgage interest, insurance, utilities, repairs, and depreciation. I never recommend this. Instead, consider the "simplified option" which simplifies the calculation and recordkeeping requirements of the allowable deduction. This allows a standard deduction of $5 per square foot of the home which is used for business, with a maximum of 300 square feet. If you have an office space which is primarily used for your writing, and you generate income from this business activity, I encourage you to explore your options of claiming a home office.

Quarterly IRS Payments: The first year of reporting new royalties, you might get away with simply paying the money due on this income when filing your taxes without penalty. However, as you continue to earn income, you are legally required to make quarterly payments to the IRS in anticipation of your annual income. Estimated payments are due in April, June, and September of the year of income, and January the year after. I typically prefer to make all payments within the same calendar year for easier tax reporting, so I submit the fourth quarterly payment before December 31.

Talk to your tax professional about the most appropriate strategy for you. Failure to make quarterly payments to the IRS while generating self-employment income can lead to undesired audits, penalties, and interest. They will know about every penny you make from online sales, be sure to report all income accurately.

Publication and Taxation as an Entity

Throughout this book, I have made numerous references to providing either an SSN or business EIN for payments and tax reporting. The intricacies of corporations, partnerships, LLCs, and sole proprietorships can quickly exceed the scope of this book. However, I would like to offer some considerations before you choose the most appropriate route for your endeavors. If you have any ambition to generate income from your writing, I highly encourage you to consider formation of some type of entity and publish through it. I personally publish through my LLC, which may be overkill for most writers. It makes sense for me because I have other business ventures under the umbrella of my LLC, but you could simplify this approach with a sole proprietorship. I believe this offers several specific benefits, as follows.

Privacy & Security: If you form a sole proprietorship with the IRS (U.S. residents), you can obtain an EIN which can be used in place of an SSN. If your EIN is leaked or breached from the service storing it, your risk of financial harm is more minimal than if you had used an SSN. If you begin to explore other income opportunities, such as paid speaking events or sales partnerships, you will be constantly asked for tax forms which have either an SSN or EIN. Handing out your SSN to strangers can have severe consequences. Providing an EIN results in much less risk.

Isolation: If you possess a full-time job with tax reporting under your SSN, you may want some official isolation from your side gig.

Taxation: In most scenarios, the overall taxes paid by a sole proprietor with an EIN should be the same as an individual using an SSN.

Professionalism: I believe providing an official sole proprietorship with IRS-issued EIN simply looks more professional than handing out your name, address, and SSN.

Contractor Status: If you begin offering consultations or paid speaking services, the client may require an EIN to justify claims that you are acting as a contractor, and not an employee.

Banking: If you plan to open a separate bank account as a sole proprietor, the bank may demand an EIN for U.S. citizens.

A sole proprietor is someone who owns an unincorporated business. There is no formation of an LLC or corporation, and taxes pass through the person through a standard 1040 tax form. A Schedule C form is added to document income and expenses. Most self-published authors operate as a sole-proprietorship. You and your writing business are one in the same. Sole-proprietorships are much simpler than an LLC or corporation. It involves no government paperwork (aside from obtaining an EIN), corporate filings, board of directors, or fees. There is no separate business tax return.

Technically, you do not need an EIN to be considered a sole proprietor. However, I do not see much point in claiming this status if you do not plan to obtain the EIN for usage on tax documents. Consult your tax professional before applying any considerations presented here. If appropriate for you, the following process obtains a sole proprietor EIN.

- Navigate to https://sa.www4.irs.gov/modiein/individual/.

- Click "Begin Application".

- Choose "Sole Proprietor" and click "Continue".

- Choose "Sole Proprietor" and click "Continue" twice.

- Choose "Started a new business" and click "Continue".

- Provide your name, SSN, and finish the process.

- Confirm all details for accuracy, as this process generates tax filing requirements.

After the application is completed, the information is validated during the online session and an EIN is issued immediately within the browser. Be sure to document any results. The online application process is only available to people located within the United States or U.S. Territories and during standard business hours.

Some authors believe they can create an LLC, elect to be taxed as an S corporation, take a small salary, and eliminate much of their self-employment taxes. Please consult with a tax professional before committing, as this injects numerous filing requirements and expenses. It also introduces a requirement to pay a reasonable salary to you and withhold FICA taxes. An S corporation only pays FICA taxes on salary compensation to its owners and not the remaining profits paid out as nontaxable dividend distributions. In my experience, this would not work and is not needed. Most royalties are already exempt from some self-employment taxation. If you have this problem, the money paid for a consultation with a tax advisor is definitely justified.

Liability

Whether you write through your own name or a sole proprietorship, you are personally responsible for any liability regarding your work. This includes copyright infringement, contract disputes, defamation, and countless other possibilities. This could place your personal assets at risk. Before you panic, let's have a reality check. The self-publishing business is not extremely risky. We are not capable of physically harming someone with our words and we are not creating dangerous explosive devices. However, writers do get sued. I have witnessed contract disputes between co-writers, trademark infringement complaints from big companies, and copyright threats from attorneys which prey on small websites. I have been issued cease and desist orders due to my own work, which fortunately did not result in civil litigation.

Many people will tell you that creating an LLC will prevent you from being liable for any damages. This is simply not true, especially if you are the sole member of the LLC. Businesses, including LLCs, get sued all of the time. Courts have found the members of the LLC liable for damages. LLC liability protection is strongest around debts incurred by the business. If you form an LLC to operate your business and do not personally guarantee or promise to pay its debts, you will likely not be personally liable for the LLC's debts. Your LLC's creditors can go after your LLC's bank accounts and other property, but they can't touch your personal property, such as your home. As a self-published author, no one is going to issue you credit, so this really does not apply.

However, if you form an LLC, you will still remain personally liable for any wrongdoing you commit during the course of your LLC business. Forming an LLC will not protect you against personal liability for your own negligence, defamation, or other personal wrongdoing. This is why I possess professional liability insurance. These policies typically cost from $400 to $1000 per year, depending on the coverage.

Some professional liability providers may want to review your work before release. I have had attorneys read my work when writing about controversial topics, which resulted in redacted content from the final publication. This requirement is rare, but may save you from legal headaches in the future.

What is best for you? Consider the amount of money you make from writing, your income tax bracket, the overall content of your work, and the likelihood of receiving unwanted legal attention due to your words. Most self-published authors obtain a sole proprietorship status, EIN from the IRS, and forego any liability insurance. Only you and your attorney or tax professional can determine the appropriate solution for your needs. Never allow me or any other online stranger to convince you to take any specific actions which could have huge legal and tax consequences.

Income & Taxes Checklist

- Monitor KDP sales.

- Monitor IngramSpark sales.

- Monitor all payments into your bank account.

- Download annual KDP tax reporting forms.

- Consider income tax deductions.

- Consider business entity formation.

- Obtain an IRS EIN (if appropriate).

- Consider professional liability insurance.

CONCLUSION

This book took a total of 160 hours to create. 123 hours were spent planning and writing; 32 hours were dedicated to editing; and 5 hours were allocated to the finishing touches and publication. My total cost for all services and products was $141.11, not including hardware and software which can be used for numerous projects. As of this writing, I have sold no copies since the book has not been published yet. However, I am eager to monitor sales and promote the content. The following was my timeline, which may be helpful to understand how I chose publication dates within various platforms.

06/01/20 - 06/18/20: Planning, notes, outlines, etc.
06/28/20 - 08/10/20: Writing
08/10/20 - 08/14/20: Editing (First draft: Self)
08/14/20 - 08/18/20: Editing (Second draft: Friendly)
08/18/20 - 08/23/20: Editing (Third draft: Professional)
08/23/20: Apply all final edits
08/23/20: Submit all files to KDP and IngramSpark
08/23/20: Order proof copy from KDP
08/29/20: Receive proof copy from KDP
08/29/20 - 09/01/20: Final proof review
09/01/20: Upload revisions and publish print version through KDP
09/15/20: Print version available on Amazon (Unexpected delay due to technical issues at KDP)
09/16/20: Publish E-book version through KDP
09/17/20: Kindle version available on Amazon
09/18/20: Publish print & E-book versions through IngramSpark

I genuinely hope that something within this book has either assisted your own journey during self-publishing or convinced you to dive in. If you would like to follow any developments of this or other projects, please visit my following online resources.

Twitter: https://twitter.com/IntelTechniques
Amazon: https://www.amazon.com/Michael-Bazzell/e/B007GNUI92
Podcast & Blog: https://inteltechniques.com

Thanks for reading. ~MB

Index

Made in the USA
Middletown, DE
29 August 2024

59961349R00119